HiRE WHO YOU WANT

Attract and **Keep** the Perfect **Employees**

JOHN HIESTER

www.Holon.co

ISBN#: 978-1-955342-66-7 (Hardback)
ISBN#: 978-1-955342-67-4 (Paperback)
ISBN#: 978-1-955342-68-1 (eBook)

Published by:

Holon Publishing & Collective Press
A Storytelling Company
www.Holon.co

Hire Who You Want

Attract and Keep the Perfect Employees

John Hiester

Holon
PUBLISHING

CONTENTS

PUBLISHER'S PREFACE

"Leslie, Leslie! Patch me in, patch me in!" I stopped Leslie mid call.

There are these pivotal moments in our lives that stand out among the rest. The kind you can count on one or two hands, if you live long enough. In those moments, we can point to single pivotal decisions that change the course of our businesses, our careers, and even our lives.

For me, one of those moments came when I stopped a new hire in the middle of a training call that I was listening in on. It was one of many routine calls with prospective authors, one of hundreds our team took together that spring. Except I knew within minutes that this call was different.

I had *one of those feelings*.

Those feelings that you get deep in your gut when you know that you must act immediately. The kind of instinctive feelings that every leader must learn to listen to, for these feelings lead to decisions that determine the fate of companies.

I knew within moments of listening to that *routine call*, on that *routine* Wednesday afternoon, that an opportunity to speak with the man on the other line was a one-in-a million opportunity. It couldn't wait until the following week, when my trainee was instructed to schedule all of the other qualified prospects on my calendar. That man was John Hiester.

I hopped on the call. An hour later, we were set. We would be reviewing a publishing contract the next day. After another 30-minute call, the plan to create and launch this book was born. *That feeling* I told you about, came with a rush and exhilaration, and an inner voice that told me, "This could be big. This could be really big. This opportunity could take your company to the next level."

That feeling was correct.

My team and I had the privilege of helping John turn his experiences and wisdom into the pages you're about to read; experience and wisdom that John has accumulated over the course of 30+ years of building his company from nothing. An organization that today, does multiple nine-figures of annual revenue, and employees hundreds of hardworking Americans.

A person does not go from working alone, making under $100k a year — to building a company that supports the lives and dreams of hundreds of families, and drives hundreds of millions of dollars a year in annual revenue — without learning a thing or two. In helping John develop the content of this book, our team received a rare education.

The real credit to helping John churn his wisdom

into the gold on these pages goes to my company's Lead Manuscript Developer, Nesha Ruther, who we had just hired when this project was taking off. However, in the months before I assigned Nesha to help John develop this life-changing book, I had weekly interviews with him to help him lay the groundwork of getting his insights on paper.

Those interviews were the equivalent of receiving top level executive coaching, which executives pay up to six-figures for. Every week I learned something new and impactful from John, which I worked to apply to my business with the same immediacy in which I took John's call. As a founder and CEO, I can tell you this: The lessons I received in helping John create this book were more valuable than an MBA. I can validate this statement with a few data points from my own company:

- Since we started working with John, the size of our team has more than *tripled*.
- While our team size grew by more than 3x, our revenue increased by 10x that year.

Yes, that's a 10 and an X. Our revenue grew by more than 1,000% in one calendar year.

We live in an economy where businesses of all shapes and sizes across the country are struggling to hire and keep their employees. Many of these businesses drive more revenue than my company does in its current state, and thus, those companies can afford to pay higher salaries and provide better benefits than my growing company can afford in 2022.

Yet, in spite of their revenue, higher salaries, matching 401k's, and superior insurance perks, they don't have what we have. We have a line out the door of people who want to work for our company, and a vigorous staff of existing A-player talent who pour their heart and soul into their work. Valuable prospects hit us up every week, asking when they can start working for us.

Every single week, even when I'm just walking around my home city of Cincinnati, someone walks up to me and asks if they can come and work for my company. They track me down, text me, DM me, and continually call my phone.

I send them to Cat, Grace, and other leaders in my organization, and they get added to the very long list of talent we will one day hire as we continue to scale. It also needs to be said that our current staff may not be with us today without the valuable lessons I learned from this book.

But, as any good entrepreneur knows, running a business is not easy. With my company's rapid growth came significant challenges and growing pains. Those growing pains were felt when our payroll for our full-time staff alone reached $40k per month, before any other business or operations expenses, and before the cost of our contractors and part-time workers.

To organizations like John's, which have *single days* in which they may gross over $1,000,000, a $40k per month payroll is nothing. To my burgeoning company, $40k per month of payroll was a giant leap forward from the tiny ship we had been just one year before.

We grew too fast.

We hired too many people!

As a result, we spent the first half of 2022 grinding to keep the lights on.

Fortunately, at the time of writing this, things have stabilized. We're making more than we did last year. Our growth is continuing, now at a healthier, steady pace.

Yet, none of that would be true without the unwavering loyalty, dedication, and commitment from our tenacious team, who endured the stress and chaos of the storm — and came out the other side with me.

But how did I know what to do when I was putting out fire after fire in the first half of the year, struggling to make payroll on time, and even struggling to *pay myself*?

The wisdom and lessons of this book were a crucial survival guide as I met my team eye to eye and said, "This is the reality of our situation. How can I better serve you as a leader?"

Thanks to John's lessons in *Hire Who You Want: Attract and Keep the Perfect Employees*, we embraced the storm, and came out stronger. Because of this book, and the incredibly valuable time I spent learning from John, I knew the proper steps to take as a leader, to keep my team motivated and charging, to continue attracting top talent, and to continue growing my company.

If you're any kind of leader in business who is looking to attract and keep the right people, to not read this book is like taking a tank of gasoline, pouring it over a few hundred grand in cash, and lighting it on fire.

For some business leaders reading this, that number will be much higher. Imagine lighting $1,000,000, $10,000,000 or even $100,000,000 on fire. That could be you, if you choose to pass on the opportunity in your hands right now.

Think of all the hardworking A-player talent who will go to work for other companies in your industry. Those companies are flourishing. They may even pay less than you. They are going to win, not because they make more than you, or have a higher percentage of market share, but because of the timeless and fundamental principles in this book.

Even if they didn't pick up and read this book, I am certain that they are already using some of the concepts and insights that this book contains.

With that said, I believe that this book has the ability to help companies across the world navigate the challenges of this post-pandemic, Great Resignation, Gig Working, Remote Working, and utterly weird economy.

Do you want to *Hire Who You Want* — and survive the coming tides?

Or do you want to settle for whomever you can

get, while other businesses in your industry collect all the top talent like Pokemon? The choice is yours.

As for myself, thanks to this book, I *Hire Who I Want.*

—Jeremy Gotwals
Founder & CEO
Holon Publishing, Ohio

FOREWORD

With 30-plus years running a large automotive group, now with nearly 500 associates, I found myself stopping my reading of *Hire Who You Want* to make notes for myself to act on the next day in the office. I have known John Hiester for several years now, and we are in a peer group together. He is a high-energy visionary that really does love people; he really does live his vision. John is an expert in his field. He has helped me improve our business and motivated me to get things done and be my best. He is unique, with an extremely high sales performance in such a small town by creating an atmosphere that draws customers from competitive markets. Honing his business practices and his company's winning culture over the past 30 years, John is often my first call or email when I need a solution.

When I read *Hire Who You Want*, I was already in agreement with John's approach toward "core values" and "loving people first." It has been my belief as well, but I was also intrigued by the easy-to-follow common sense steps he lays out that are often missed. For example, John talks about the interview process he has developed with his management team. This has been an area of weakness in my company. As soon as I finished the chapter, I developed a training course with our HR manager to implement John's process with our leadership. There are many more useful methods John shares in this book. I am excited for you to read *Hire Who You Want* and to use it as an operational guide. Whether you are just getting started on your entrepreneurial journey, are years into building your business, or you have always wanted to take a leap toward living your core values every day but don't know how to start or keep it going, this book will give you the roadmap. John has shared what it takes to be different, to be better, and to live your values, while becoming more successful than you dare to put in writing.

—Tim Dagenais
President & COO
Tony Group, Hawaii

INTRODUCTION

In today's landscape, it's becoming increasingly evident that the acquisition of talent is the most valuable skill that leaders can have within an organization. The workplace dynamic is changing, and unemployment is reaching all-time highs. The problems businesses are facing now are the same ones they have always faced, just more extreme. What I mean by that is that the talent pool is shrinking as unemployment goes up. Capturing true talent and knowing how to develop and keep that talent is becoming more and more important every day.

Seeing so many businesses struggling to acquire and retain talent, I reflected on my own practices at Hiester Automotive. I have known for a long time that our methods, while unconventional, have the power to be transformative. It was in this moment of economic instability, however, that I realized business owners needed our insights more than ever. I chose to write this book because I truly believe I have something to offer, a new perspective on what it means to hire and attract talent, and how to give your employees what they need to stay so that you experience less turnover.

In 2001, I purchased my first store, a little dealership on a back road in Angier, North Carolina, a town of about 2,000 people. It was an instant success. We probably did close to a million in sales that year with roughly 20 employees. And over the last 18 years, I have taken that business and grown it to an annual income of over 20 times that first year's revenue. We now have four locations: Sanford, Fuquay, and two in Lillington. We also bought a parts distribution business; we have a large ACDelco distributorship and have 16 trucks on the road delivering batteries to dealerships around the state. And, of course, we have smaller businesses that are ancillary to that business.

Our success has been well documented. We have won several awards, and I have had opportunities to speak and share how I have built my business. I am at a place in my life where my business is still expanding, but I am looking to give back. I want to give back by sharing my experiences and allowing the next generation of entrepreneurs to learn not only from our successes, but from the mistakes we have made along the way as well.

In our circles, we are revered for the unique nature of how we do things. I want to share that knowledge. No matter your field, you are likely facing a shortage of high-performing talent. Yet despite how crucial this element is, a lot of businesses leave it up to chance. They spend a lot of money managing day-to-day operations and marketing their business, but they don't put the effort into systematically approaching one of their most valuable commodities, which is their people.

I published my first book, *Why Jacob Matters*, in 2019, which follows the story of my employee Jacob and what he taught me about successful leadership. In this book as well, I will use stories and anecdotes from my years of managing to illustrate points and convey ideas.

My intent with this book is to give you the tools to prioritize your people, and in doing so, make your business attractive to potential hires. I like to illustrate these lessons through stories, the true stories of mistakes that we've made and successes that we've had. My hope is that you will learn how best to support your team so they can help your business thrive. I have over 300 employees, which means my business is over 300% larger than it was when it began. Yet through a process of curated practices and leadership tactics, it now only takes 10% of my time to manage them. It may sound hard to believe, but the larger my business has gotten, the less time it takes to manage. This is, and always will be, because I prioritize my employees.

> *It may sound hard to believe, but the larger my business has gotten, the less time it takes to manage. This is, and always will be, because I prioritize my employees.*

Whether you are a seasoned business owner facing the hiring challenges that are affecting our nation, a small-business owner trying to scale, or an aspiring entrepreneur looking for a sign to take the leap, this book is for you. Many business owners are hesitant to share their insights, successes, and failures. They have a vested interest in maintaining the secrecy around how they run and maintain a successful business. As you will see through the course of this book, that is not my belief.

Over the course of the following nine chapters, I will break down how my company goes about acquiring talent, from placing ads to the interview process. I will explain the infrastructure we built to ensure employees have everything they need to stay with us. And I will reveal the stories of trial and error that got my business to where it is today.

Over the last two decades, Hiester Automotive has developed practices that allow my employees to perform better, build workplace morale, and create an environment that attracts the kind of quality talent that is so in demand. These practices have altered my business for the better, and I believe they will do the same for yours.

—John Hiester
Cary, North Carolina

SUPPLEMENTAL MATERIALS

This book was designed to give readers all the tools and information they need to create hiring practices to secure and retain talent. At the end of each chapter, you will find a QR code.

These QR codes are linked to supplemental materials relating to the content of the chapter. These materials include videos, exercises, and examples of some of our long-standing practices here at Hiester Automotive. We hope these materials will aid you and your business for years to come.

To access the content available through the QR code, simply take your phone's camera and hover over the code. A link will emerge to direct you to the page. Click on it, and you're good to go!

CHAPTER 1

HIRE WHO YOU WANT

My wife and I went to dinner last night, and the restaurant we went to was almost empty. There were probably 12 or 13 tables that were seated between the outside patio and the inside dining room. The rest of it just looked like a ghost town. However, when we went to the maître d', they said there was a 15-minute wait. I looked around and said, "15-minute wait, you say?"

"Well, because we don't have staff, 'cause of staffing issues."

I'm thinking to myself, you need this book more than I do because the truth is that the staff is out there, you just don't know how to fish for them. You're like a fisher that's got a hook with no bait on it.

Using the restaurant business as an example,

what are the things that are stopping people from applying for a job as a waiter? Are they wary of having to rely on tips? Does the restaurant not have a positive reputation? Are they anxious about serving customers? Is the rate you're paying not generating enough income so that they can live?

Whatever your business may be, you need to identify what attracts people, and what serves as barriers of entry. You have to step back and utilize your own intelligence and the intelligence of your group and ask, "What are the reasons people aren't attracted to this right now?" Once those reasons are clearly identified, the real work begins. This is when you roll up your sleeves and say, "Okay, let's think outside the box. How can we make this business attractive to our target audience?" It starts there.

> *The truth is the staff is out there, you just don't know how to fish for them. You're like a fisher that's got a hook with no bait on it.*

The reason why is simple. Your people determine your success in business. If you are in a position where you need to hire people, understanding how to attract the right people saves you money, makes you money, and builds your business.

Companies spend billions of dollars on recruitment to attract talent to their business. Yet talent is not the only quality employers need to be looking for.

There needs to be a conversation about how that talent fits into the larger culture of your business. When you are attracting employees solely based on talent, people become transient. They come for a period, and then they move on to the next highest bidder. The expense this creates in your company is astronomical.

According to a Society for Human Resource Management (SHRM) report from June 16th, 2020, the average cost to a company for employee turnover is $3,500 per employee. The average cost for annual training is $1,500 per employee. These statistics are imperative in understanding why acquiring and retaining talent can mean the difference for your business. According to SHRM, not only is it expensive to hire and expensive to train, but the average person in their first month of employment performs at 25% of the capacity that they will have when they are totally engaged in their job. In weeks 5–12 of employment, that performance reaches 50% of their capacity. What that means is that in the first 12 weeks of a new hire's employment, you are only getting 25-50% of the capacity of your previous employee, assuming they were a quality employee. At weeks 13–20, you get about 75%. Even up to 20 weeks, you are still getting 25% less capacity than you were receiving with your previous employee.

When thinking about the cost to re-hire, you should ask yourself, "How much time should I take to make the right decision on hiring this employee?" Factoring in all of these statistics, it is so much more economical to take your time hiring than to make a hasty and potentially wrong decision. The bottom line is that people are solving the problems that are right in front of them rather than proactively taking the time to identify what great looks like. You need to define what great looks like for the position you are trying to fill before you ever meet with candidates. People should be working towards greatness instead of responding to the problems that emerge through-out the day with reactionary hiring and management practices, because it ends up costing you 10 times the time and money as it would to do it right the first time.

Imagine what your company could do if you nev-er had to worry about attracting and maintaining the right people. If you never had employees leave unex-pectedly or had to find rushed replacements? What would your company be able to accomplish if you could rely on a consistent body of high-performing talent and could trust that the right people for your company would find you?

The way to accomplish this is to not go into hiring blindly. The tools you need are already at your dispos-al. If you have attracted the right people in the past, and you have managed them the way they deserve to be managed, they can help you attract more talent.

The difference between great employees and average employees is that great employees are con-stantly trying to figure out how to make your busi-ness better. They are constantly working towards a common mission. And the reason they can do this is that they have the security and the freedom to do so. They have confidence in what they are doing and who they are doing it for, so they can think outside the box. They will come up with ideas in ways you had never even thought of to make the business better.

What I am trying to accomplish with this book is to provide you with a map to finding quality talent. The map is the key. How do you get the right people within the right seats in our company? You have to take the time to identify what great looks like. That way when you are going out into the market looking for the person to fill a position, you already know what you are looking for. Not just in job function, but in core values as well. That is how you—and I— find the people that fit the company and accomplish the tasks that are set in front of them.

THE FOUR FUNDAMENTALS

The Four Fundamentals of Employee Engagement are critical to how we run our business and maintain a culture that continues to attract new talent. The idea is that every employee within our company should be able to answer "yes" to the following questions:

- **Does what I do matter?** Is my work fulfilling? Does it impact the overall culture of the company?
- **Do I have a voice?** In other words, "If I have an idea or a problem, is there going to be some-

body there that'll listen to me and respect my opinion?"

- **Am I growing?** Do I see a path to success through my current position?
- **Am I fairly compensated?** Well, when it comes to hiring people, I think you can eliminate the last question right up front. When you answer yes, you're one step closer to attracting talent.

It's my belief that if a person can answer yes to the first three questions, then the fourth one becomes less important. But if a person can't answer yes to the first three questions, then the fourth is the only one that matters. If I come to work for you, how can you determine if I feel like I matter, or if I feel like I have a voice?

It's simple. Look in their eyes in the morning. If they are excited and eager to face the day, you know they feel like they matter. If they come to you with ideas and thoughts, and if you take the time to listen to and incorporate those ideas, they will feel like they have a voice. But if they constantly come to you with ideas and you never take the time to speak with them, or you never try to implement their thoughts, then they are probably not going to be able to answer yes to that second question.

Sometimes it is the little things that we miss in our day-to-day operations that sets an employee down a path that is not right for them or for us. When an employee comes to our organization, we want them to grow. We want to invest in them so whether they stay with us for a year, 10 years, or the rest of their lives, the experience caused them to grow individually, spiritually, mentally, and developmentally.

The structure of our meetings and daily huddles are designed to put management in a position to look in their employees' eyes each and every day. They are designed to make our employees feel important. Because if I matter to you, you will matter to me. As a leader, you need to matter to your employees. You need them to feel that you can take them to a level they can't get to on their own. The way you do that is by investing in them. How do you invest in them? You take the time to stop what you're doing and listen.

When an employee first comes to work for your organization, you are trying to get to know them. You will ask them questions and share information about the business with them. But once they are engaged in their job, we tend to take advantage of that and say, "Go do your job," and we move on to the next thing. But what made them feel so good about their job when they first started working was that they felt like they mattered. But once you move on, and you feel as if you have already shared everything with them, you start to ignore them. That is the moment where they get off track.

Every relationship you have is always within your control. And if something goes wrong, it usually hinges on either something you did or didn't do. When you hire someone and you think they are the right person, they are engaged and doing great work, but all of a sudden, they might get off track. The first thing we tend to do as managers is accuse them of slacking off and give them more direction. But the truth is, as leaders, we need to figure out why they don't have the same vigor they did when they first arrived. How can we course correct so they can not only do their job, but excel at their job and help build the success of our company?

Using the Four Fundamentals, you can look back at any situation in your life and see what you did or did not do in order for you to end up in this position. Hopefully, you can catch it early enough that you can right the ship. How do you right the ship? Stop what you are doing and let that person feel important to you, spend a little time with them. I like to share with my employees things that are going on in the company, or exciting upcoming news, even if that news is irrelevant to their position. This allows the employee to feel like they are a part of the community at large and know they have a role in the exciting projects down the line. What you will see from doing that is it will put the person in a position to answer "yes" to the rest of the questions.

Am I growing? Well, if you listen and share with an employee, they will ask questions about opportunities. And quite frankly, you will like them more and begin considering them for more opportunities.

In those sessions where you take the time to make them feel like they matter, you are going to share methods of growth. You will start saying, "We do X because of Y," instead of simply telling them to do X.

Do I have a voice? There are times when people within my organization will come to me with a thought or an idea, and when you're busy and your business is doing well, it is easy to plow through and stay the course. But the truth is that the world is changing. The way people think and communicate is changing. If an employee in my organization comes to me with a thought, and I never take the time to consider it and incorporate it into how we do business, that employee is never going to come to me again. So often I see early and entry-level managers feel like they need to be an expert when an employee comes to them. While they should certainly have the knowledge to answer questions and address concerns, they also have to be open to new ideas. When an employee comes to me and I incorporate their idea, it ties them to the business. They feel like they contributed to the success of the business, and it causes them to want to contribute more.

The difference between a leader and a manager is asking your employees the Four Fundamentals and having them answer yes.

Am I fairly compensated? If they contribute at a high level and they are advancing the success of our business, they are going to be fairly compensated. What I have found is that when people take their eye off the money and focus on the contribution, the money gets bigger than they ever would have dreamed. I can tell you of several cases within our company right now where our employees are living a life they never thought they would be able to live. It has also been my experience that when a focus is solely on money, the company doesn't work. The dollar should be a trophy for a job well done, not the reason we do what we do.

Through reading this book, I hope you can put yourself in a position where you know that every employee you are responsible for can answer yes to those four questions. You can accomplish so much more when every player on your team is playing at the maximum of their abilities, rather than resting on what you alone can do.

BUILD CULTURE

What many people don't realize about the hiring process is how much work is required on your end. Sure, the prospective employees have to put their best foot forward, but you have to sell them on your vision. You have to make a commitment to them that they will be better off working for you than for anyone else. I have said it before and I will say it again, your people determine your success in business. If you're in a position where you need to hire people, understanding how to attract the right people saves you money, makes you money, and builds your business.

Everything in our company comes down to our community culture. Nothing is an individual practice. And culture is not something you can buy or get. It's something that grows, it's something you build. You can't just decide you are going to have a good culture today. The culture of your company is your people. If you are wondering what your company culture looks like, look at your employees.

> *Everything in our company comes down to our community culture. Nothing is an individual practice.*

How do they interact with customers? How do they interact with one another? Do they feel comfortable coming to you with questions, problems, and ideas? Are they working towards their own individual success or the success of the company? These are all indicators of your company's culture.

If you've taken the time to identify what great looks like, you've hired people that embody those characteristics, you engage them in day-to-day activity, and you invest in them and value them, then your culture is automatically going to develop itself. You will find you organically have a group of people working towards a common goal. And that, my friends, is what will win over your potential hires.

When I say hire who you want, what I mean is build the company that will attract the people you want. Build a culture that your ideal employees will want to be a part of.

Throughout this book, you will hear me mention our core values. These values are at the root of our company culture and drive everything we do, including hiring. Everyone we hire has to embody these core values. They are as follows:

- Character/Integrity
- Loves People
- Possess a Get-It-Done Attitude
- Professionalism
- Possess a Servant Attitude

THE EMPLOYEE IS ALWAYS RIGHT

One example of a change I created in our culture was this age-old mantra: The customer is always right. Make no mistake, I believe in serving the needs of our customers. But as far as the culture of my business goes, I want everyone to understand that the employee is always right. I think many times in business, managers and leaders fail to understand that if an employee was right for the job when hired, they likely still are. If they are successful in their day-to-day operations and all of a sudden, an issue emerges, the issue is typically not their fault.

Your job as a manager isn't to stick them in a corner and say, "Do your job." Your job is to figure out what the problem is, understand why the employee is falling short, and try to feel the way they do. You need to change the system so that the employee can continue to succeed. This is what I mean when I say the employee is always right. And the truth is that having a culture where your employees know they are protected, where they know you are on their side, is going to be a lot more appealing to prospective hires than a culture that discards them the second they mess up.

> *Many times in business, managers and leaders fail to understand that if an employee was right for the job when hired, they likely still are.*

For years and years, I worked in an organization where what was right didn't matter, value mattered. In other words, if an employee makes a lot of money, they matter, and we listen to them. If an employee just fills a void, "Do your job and get paid," they don't matter, and we don't listen to them. If a customer complained, the situation would be handled by appeasing the customer and punishing the employee. Unfortunately, that is the kind of workplace that is often created by the "customer is always right" mentality.

In my company, we attract people who fit our organization, we establish an outline of what a successful job looks like from the very beginning, we measure employee success, and we praise them as they advance. Because of this, our employees always want to please the customer. If they ever get out of line with a customer, it causes me to stop and figure out where I failed them.

What happened? I know my employees won't be rude to customers unless the customer is being horrible to them, and in that case, I or a manager will step in. I love my employees and I don't want them to be abused. And when my employees know they are protected, I don't have to worry about them. They know they don't have to make themselves miserable trying to make sure the customer is always right. Instead, they can perform their best, knowing in the eyes of the company, the employee is always right.

One of the things that I think is an issue in the world today is that we put too much value in the position that somebody's in and not enough value in what is right. In our business, every manager in our organization knows that I am always going to defend what is right. What you do for my company and how much money you make my company doesn't mean anything to me because I'm not doing this for the money.

When it comes to a dispute, every single employee in this organization needs to know that we're always going to defend what is right. If a manager is doing something wrong, you have more power as an entry-level broom sweeper than you do if you're a CEO. Everyone, no matter their salary, is beholden to that code.

RIGHT RULES

The most critical thing you can do as a manager is to be attentive to the needs of your employees. Once you know what someone is looking to get out of a workplace, and you can guarantee those things, you will be attractive to the great employees you are looking for.

You cannot go into hiring blindly. You don't just drop an ad that says, "Fishermen needed," you run an ad that's specific to what you want and specific to what you can provide. More than likely, if you attract the right people into your business, and you've managed them attentively, they'll help you attract more people.

I have all kinds of people working for me at Hiester Automotive, including my friends and family. Sometimes this raises eyebrows, but I have no problem hiring my loved ones. I'll give a good example as to why.

One of my sales managers was having trouble managing a relative of mine and fired them. The sales manager came to me beforehand. He told me the employee was behaving poorly, and he didn't know what to do. I said, "Well, why would you allow them to do that? It's not in their best interest or your best interest for them to talk to you that way. You need to look them in the eye and say, 'Maybe this isn't the place for you.'"

I give every person in this company full support.

We're not a top-down management style, we're really closer to a bottom-up. Right always rules in our business. My love for you should be felt in the way that I hold you accountable, not in my allowance of you to be outside the law because of your relationship with anybody or your position. Neither of those matters in our company at all. I believe that right rules. Why do I care whether you're a friend or a relative or anything else? I'm going to hold you to the same standard that I'm going to hold anybody else to. So, yes, I have employees in my company that are relatives or friends. If you're proud of what you do, and you are true to what you do, then why wouldn't you want to recruit and attract people that you love and care about, whether they're relatives or friends?

I tell my employees this right up front: "Please know, my way to this thing is whether you're a general manager or you're on the clean-up line, you both have the same authority when it comes to issues on right or wrong, period. Your 10-year experience doesn't make you above the law."

I have cousins that work here. I have a son-in-law that works here. I have a daughter's boyfriend that works here, some of my best friends work here, and they work here because they want some of what we've got. They want to be a part of it. Why would I deprive them of that because of their bloodline or their heritage or their friendships?

If you're not strong enough to manage high-performance people, then don't do it. I expect the best from my employees and hold their behavior to a set of standards, no matter our relationship.

Weak managers allow people to continue behavior that's not in their best interest long-term. For us, we look at it and say, "Character and integrity are our core values." Character and integrity are first because if you can't trust somebody, you can't lead them, and if they can't trust you, they're not going to follow you.

This is the key: I'd rather manage somebody I have to hold back than hire somebody I have to kick. Our mission is to love and inspire people to become the best that they can be. The idea is we want them to be the very best, but it also requires a desire on the part of the employee to grow and learn. If they don't have that, if they think they can treat people poorly, they need to know it won't be tolerated. When I make a decision for an employee, or one of my managers makes a decision for an employee, it's in their best interest, not just in mine. Therefore, allowing bad behavior is not in the best interest of the employee who is doing it, but also everyone they interact with.

> **I'd rather manage somebody I have to hold back, than hire somebody I have to kick.**

I believe loving people is holding them accountable in the same way that a great coach pulls your helmet down right in front of everybody and says, "Hey, you've got to get down here, not up there," because what's happening is you're allowing the whole system to break down. My way of thinking is that if you continue in the behavior or put Band-Aids on it, you're not fixing your issues, and you're not growing. Loving people isn't roses and candy. Loving people is looking at them as if they're your child and thinking, "For their future, is allowing them to continue this behavior in their best interest?"

Loving people is: "I care so much about you that even if I'm going to lose you as an employee, I am willing to take that chance because you mean that much to me. And I know that if I allow you to continue in the behavior you're exhibiting, it's going to lead to a lesser future for you."

Right rules in our company. No matter if you are a friend or a relative. That is how I show my employees that I love them. My employees know if they are behaving poorly, I love them enough to tell them the truth and hold them accountable. They know if someone is treating them badly, I love them enough to defend them and not let anything go unchecked.

If you think about it, "Am I growing?" can't be answered honestly if you're allowed to work outside the lines, or if you're allowed to slack off on a section of the business or a part of your job responsibilities. How do you ensure that doesn't happen? Through establishing agreed-upon measurables for everyone involved. It is very difficult to help an employee answer yes to that question if you don't have accurate measurables in place to illustrate that growth.

As people working together, we need to agree on how that work is going to be conducted. The message, vision, and measurables need to be clear. If those things are established, then I shouldn't have any problem looking you in the eye and saying:

"Look, not allowed here. Not acceptable. We agreed on this. You're the one breaking the agreement, not me. This is what you said you'd do, this is what you're going to do, or I'm going to help you find a job somewhere else." It may seem like tough love, but establishing measurables for the kind of behavior you want from your employees and holding them to those standards allows them to succeed.

One of the things that I talk about when I'm training people to hire others is this: You have got to recognize that the person you're getting ready to hire is not somebody you're trying for a position. I am not someone who just tries anything. I either go all in, or I don't do it at all. I never hire with the intention to try someone for a position; when I hire someone, I want it to be forever. This is somebody I'm expecting to be in a family with, to have a relationship with for the rest of my life. I know a lot of people that haven't experienced that kind of culture are going to look at that and say, "Well, look, I got a job, I got a ditch I got to get dug, I need bodies in that ditch, and this is all frou-frou and fluffy."

But this method of hiring creates a culture that is

so unique and so sought after in my business. Whoever I choose to hire, I want them to have everything they need to stay on for the rest of their career. The goal is to form a long-lasting relationship with them, and so I treat it as such. While this mentality may seem unnecessary to some, it has ensured that I always have high-quality talent working for my company, and I don't have to live in fear of a valued employee leaving.

I had a conversation the other day with somebody that we were promoting.

I said, "Okay, you've been here for two years, you've experienced it. You've got the opportunity to move to the next level, but I need you to understand something with every fiber in your body. If you're going to take this position, which I think you've earned the right to have, know that if you take it and you're not 100% committed to it, you're taking an opportunity from somebody else to grow in their career. Forget about yourself for a minute and know that. You either have to be all in, stay where you're at, or do something else. You have got to be all in."

I told him not to answer me right now, but to think about it. I treat every employee as a part of a commitment that affects our entire company. If a person we choose to promote is not all in, he is limiting the other candidates. I want my employees to know they are making the same commitment to me as I have made to them. If we are going to be part of a family together, I want them to make the right decisions, for the right reasons.

PREDETERMINED VICTORY

Ben Stein has a quotation I live by: "The indispensable first step to getting what you want out of life is this: decide what you want." The idea is that any time we go into a hiring situation, whether it be a new position or an existing position, there has to be a predetermined victory. There has to be a predetermined understanding of who we're looking for and how we're looking for it.

What is the interviewer's role in it? Well, they're an extension of me and you. They are acting as a representative of the company's leadership. They have to know what they want before they even enter the interview. Before we go into a single interview, we sit down as a team and identify very clearly what we want. We ask, what are the most important parts of this job, and what qualities do we need to fulfill those parts of the job? If it's a data input job, we need someone who's very accurate; they need to have a keen eye for detail. If it's a customer-facing job, we need someone who is charismatic. We ask, what are the primary tasks going to be? Where are the places where people are struggling with this position right now? What deficiencies do we have now that this position could help solve? We will also look inward to find what we want from someone coming in from the outside. Who is the best at that position right now? What qualities make them so good at it? Once we've identified those qualities, we now know we want to hire someone who has more of those same qualities.

I have a good story about why this process is so important. One of the things that is changing in our industry is that the supply chain has been disrupted. There is a shortage of industry both in parts and sales. Because we're an innovative company, we decided to centralize our buying years ago. This meant we had to create a new buyer's position, so we sat down and tried to figure out what skills were needed for this job.

This person needed to have enough knowledge of the car business to differentiate between models very quickly. They had to be skilled at research and be able to type at least 80 words a minute. It had to be someone who could sit behind a desk for a long period of time, so maybe not someone who was looking for a highly interactive job.

What we realized through this process was that we actually knew the perfect candidate. We had a kid work for us as a salesman who was a total savant, as smart as anyone in our company about product knowledge. He had a really strong passion for automobiles. He also knew data. I've been in this business for 30 years and this kid blows me away on product knowledge. But he struggled with face-to-face customer interaction. He was fine when it came to online communication. He fit our core values to a T, he just struggled with speaking directly to customers. We had to let him go as a salesman because that ability is crucial to a salesman position. It was never going to work.

But when we identified what we wanted for this new buyer's position, we thought, "Holy crap. This kid is perfect for this position." We needed someone skilled with technology, someone who was data-wise. He used to shoot YouTube videos for us because he loved computer functions so much; he was just made for this job. With an online buyer, you need someone that can process a lot of data through vAuto and CARFAX all in a timely fashion, and then send customers an offer. We would never have considered him had it not been crystal clear exactly what we needed. He came in to test out the position and blew us all away.

We put together a road map before anyone ever comes in for an interview. We do this so that we never lower our standards and accept something less than what we need. If you know what you need from the beginning, it's impossible to fail because you won't accept anything less than excellent, and you will never end up disappointed. It also ensures the employee is set up for success. If you hire someone based on a job description that is entirely different from what they end up doing, you can't be upset if they struggle, you can't be upset if they aren't accomplishing what you wanted them to because you have set them up to fail. We want to make sure it's a predetermined success both for ourselves and for the employee.

One exercise I do when I am training hiring

managers is I bring the team together and highlight the prerequisites for a certain position. As a team, we go over the qualities that would make someone the perfect candidate for this job. Then I bring in a superstar, a really high-performing employee, and I ask the team, "Would you hire him for this position? Would he be a good fit?"

Now everyone in the room knows and loves this employee. They ad-

> *If you hire someone based on a job description that is entirely different from what they end up doing, you can't be upset if they struggle.*

mire him, they know he is a high performer, and so most people say, "Yes. No question about it. We would hire him." But if the position says this employee needs to be computer savvy, and they need to be able to type 120 words a minute, the responsibilities of this job don't match this person because this employee isn't computer savvy or a fast typer. We love this employee, he is great at his job, but all of a sudden, we realize he is not a perfect candidate for the job we were originally talking about.

What this exercise does is it trains our hiring managers in the importance of knowing up front what they are looking for in an employee. Without clear prerequisites, you end up hiring based on other factors. You hire because you like the candidate, you respect them, and see their good qualities. But if they don't meet the expectations of the job, you end up trying to fit a square peg into a round hole.

I listen to a lot of audiobooks, and one of the books I'm listening to is *Start With Why* by Simon Sinek. He shares a story about two Japanese auto manufacturers he works with. There was a door that didn't fit properly into the vehicle. The first auto manufacturer's general manager puts a guy on the assembly line, and his job is to take a mallet and make the door line up with the fender so it fits.

Well, the second auto manufacturer redesigned the door so it fits the car. It takes more labor and costs more money, but at the end of the day, everything is assembled the correct way. And the way he phrases it is that everything is made either "by design or by default." If you are using the mallet to make the door fit, it fits by default. If you redesign the door so it is made to fit the car, it is by design.

And the truth is, 80% to 90% of people who are hiring talent are hiring by default. They identify the job description and write it down, but they don't take the time to envision what their ideal employee is like. They don't get specific, and they certainly don't run the employee by their core values. Most people, when they have a vacancy or an opportunity in their company, only create an idea of what they want in their mind and then interview people. And as they sit there in the interview room, they have the mallet in their hand, and they are trying to figure out how to make that candidate fit their job.

It happens to everybody. You have a vacancy you are eager to fill. If you don't fill the position, you are going to have to do the work yourself. As soon as you see someone you like, you start hammering away trying to make them fit. You see the good in that person, and you are trying to expand upon it to justify putting them in that position. It doesn't mean the applicant doesn't have good qualities. It just means you are trying to make them fit, and if the fit was perfect, you wouldn't have to justify it.

You think to yourself, "Well, we'll try it." I never want to try anybody. I never want to put someone in a position unless I am certain they are made for that position. When I hire people, I want to change their life. I want to inspire them to be all that they can be. And I can't do that if I'm trying to shove a square peg in a round hole. In my experience, when you establish what great looks like, great appears. When you design the position with your ideal candidate in mind, down to the specifics, that person will show up. When you don't know what great looks like, you settle for what you get.

> **When you don't know what great looks like, you settle for what you get.**

All of my employees know this, and because we've established what this person should be up front, if somebody gets hired who is not that, we know we have a problem on the managerial level. I can sit down with whoever did the hiring and say, "Okay, we established what perfect was. When you interviewed this person, did they check this off? Did they check that off? If so, why the change?"

In my businesses, we've put systems in place to make sure this doesn't happen. We have an accountability partner present throughout the interview process. This is someone who has been vetted and trained by me to make the final decision. In our stores, this role is filled by the general manager. They interview the candidate and make the final decision. We want everybody to grow and to have increased responsibility. But in our eyes, there is nothing more important than who is brought into the company. It's the most important thing.

We are very selective about who makes the final decision about whether someone is hired or not. And they have to be accountable to me for it. If a mistake has been made, I don't go to the department head and say, "Why did you hire this person?" I go directly to the general manager and say, "Hey, here are the qualities the candidate was supposed to have. Clearly, this person is not right, so what happened?"

The worst answer a manager can give me in that situation is "Oh, I wasn't there for the interview." Then we have a problem because I need to know this is as much a priority for the managers as it is for me. Sometimes, I'll see people start squirming to say, "Oh, well, you know." And then I know they screwed up.

That's when you must be upfront and say, "Can you see why this is so important? It isn't about the job, it's about everyone around them who now must work with someone who is unqualified for the job you gave them." In order to have a predetermined victory, every member of the hiring process must understand its importance. Everyone needs to buy into the vision.

A PURE VISION

There's a business metaphor I like about Michelangelo looking at David. When you think about the sculpture of David, the way he looks in that statue is exactly the way Michelangelo saw him in his mind. If Michelangelo saw David with scars, David would have had scars. But he didn't see him with scars, and that's why there aren't there in the end product. With magical artists like Michelangelo, what you have is a vision that is so pure, they can carve out of stone exactly what they see in their mind.

When you get a vision clear in your mind, your whole life is about that vision. Everything in your life starts to be in service of making that vision a reality. Whenever I go into a meeting where there are going to be negotiations or evaluations, I like to identify what exactly it is that I want to come out of that negotiation. It's the same practice as identifying what I want in a prospective employee.

David Anderson says, "If you're struggling to hire people, look who is doing your hiring." A mediocre employee is not going to be able to hire a great one. A mediocre employee is certainly not going to be able to mentor a great one. Nobody gets to be a manager in my company without being excellent in their own right. But they are also trained in accordance with my vision and the core values of the company.

When I look at my managers, they need to be trained to the point where my vision for the company is crystal clear in their mind, so clear they could carve it out of stone. What they do on a day-to-day basis should be a perfect enactment of the vision I have given them. That's why it is so easy to tell when something goes wrong in my company, because the standard I hold them to is so high, and they fulfill it so consistently that anything less is obvious.

Going into the hiring process, my managers understand their role. Their role is not to decide whether they like or dislike the other person in the room. Their job is to come in and say, "Does this person check off the things on our list that we want for this position?" It is very common for whoever is interviewing a candidate to fall in love with them. Nobody works for my company who doesn't love people anyway. They fall in love with the candidate and start trying to figure out how they can sell this person regardless of whether or not they meet the qualifications. That's why I have a second party come in and double-check all new hires to make sure they really fit our core values and meet all of the qualifications. And while I won't say it's foolproof, it does weed out 99% of the mistakes.

When we talk about hiring who you want, you have to know who you want to hire before you do it. You have got to see it in your mind. I'm not talking about physical appearance. Discrimination in any form is not tolerated in our hiring practices – nor should it be in yours. I'm talking about it from a character and behavioral standpoint. Every aspect of the ideal candidate needs to be clear enough that you could put it on paper or carve it out of stone. We try to look at every aspect of the position because we don't want managers, we want artists. We want people who know so clearly what great looks like that the product is exactly like it was in their mind.

I do this in every part of my business. We use this company called Car Wars, and what they do is they have people listen to our calls with customers to see if they check certain things off the list, and when something isn't checked off, they send us a notification. My expectation is that my managers listen to those calls to see where the imperfections are. And what I hate to hear them say is "It was pretty good." What's pretty good? Either it was the way we designed it, or it wasn't. And if it wasn't and you're accepting it as "pretty good," then we have a problem. There is a right way and a wrong way. That is how you ensure your vision is translated, by making sure there are only two options: right or wrong.

SELL THE VISION

I hear people say all the time that they are struggling to find talented employees. The skilled trades are disappearing, and there is a small pool of quality employees. There are a million reasons why you aren't hiring quality employees. But there have always been a million reasons.

Any great sales organization knows the difference between making and missing a sale is the energy the customer feels from the person doing the selling. What these great organizations teach their employees is that how confident and excited you are is often all it takes to make a sale. Somebody that had no interest in buying may decide to do so purely because the salesman is excited about the product.

If you are marketing a product, what is it that makes advertising effective? Effective advertising makes the customer feel like their life will be better if they have this product. It makes customers want to do business with you because they trust you, they find you inspiring, they are excited by you, and believe the things you do bring value to their life on some level. It is all interrelated. If you apply those same principles to attracting and hiring talent, you can't help but win.

Let's translate that to an interview setting; notice what the person doing the interview sounds like when they sit in front of that prospective employee. Are they inspiring? Are they creating confidence? Are they exhibiting the energy to motivate a decision? Do they believe in the product? This is one of the main points I am trying to convey with this book. If you are struggling to hire talent, look at who is during the hiring. Make sure that person is so energized about the vision the company has for this position, that the person in front of them has no choice but to want to come to work for you.

I don't want employees who are simply working here because they want a paycheck. I want employees who work here because they believe in the vision, and they want to be a part of where it is going. If you can sell people on that vision, if you can get them to believe in it, everything in your company will relate back to it. We don't do what we do on a daily basis because it needs to be done, we do it because it moves us closer to our common goal. When that idea is embedded in the heart and soul of everyone who works for you, it becomes part of everything they do. When someone applies for a job, I want them to understand that vision and go out and sell it to the world.

When my managers finally enter the interview room the first time they meet the candidates, their job is to sell the vision of our company to the prospective employee. At the same time, they have to evaluate the person to make sure that they fit our core values first. They have to make sure that they crossed everything off the list.

Here's why it matters. Right now, restaurants all over my town are closing because they can't hire staff to fill the positions. And yet, my daughter opened a bakery-cafe during the pandemic and is fully staffed. She has hired three servers in the last two months because of the growth that she's experienced.

When I was young and working for another organization, I worked for less money, I worked crazy hours, and I gave my heart and soul to my work because I believed in the vision. I felt like I was a part of something. When I spoke, management listened. People are willing to commit when they feel they are a part of a brand, an identity. Think about how sports fans will live and die by their team. It's not really about the players, or how well or poorly they perform, it is about the feeling of community people have with other fans and with the team itself. If you identify a cohesive brand and make your employees feel a part of it, they will dedicate themselves to ensuring its success.

This is how I know that if your vision is strong enough, people are going to come to work for you. Even if they can make more money elsewhere, they will come to work for you because people want to do a job, they feel is meaningful. I have seen that behavior over and over again in myself and my employees. If you are struggling to hire, it is likely because you haven't communicated the vision of your business and why that prospective employee's work will matter. The prospective hire should leave that interview room thinking, "How can I NOT go work for that company?"

Once, a friend of mine called me one afternoon and he told me that he was struggling to attract talent. He gave me an example of a kid that was working at the bus garage, making $18 an hour, but could make more money working for him. "But the guy doesn't take the job," he says, "because his girlfriend wants to have the security of a government job." And he went on to say, "I feel like I had the wrong person there."

I said, "Well, I don't think you had the wrong person there." He was understandably confused, so I told him: "Let me ask you a question. Do you think if he was excited enough by your vision he wouldn't have been able to convince his girlfriend why he needed to do it? Or did he use his girlfriend as an excuse for why he didn't take the job?"

Oftentimes if people leave your business or decide not to take a position, they will be polite and give you an excuse that allows you to think it is not about you. They will say someone else paid better, or they wanted to work closer to their home, and those things could all be true. But if you can convince someone to become part of your vision, they will be willing to make those sacrifices. Most of the time, if you want to get to the root of the problem, you have to look back and determine, where did you lose?

Did you show him that if he hooked his cart to your train, what he did was going to matter? Did you show him he was going to have a voice in the company, he was going to see an opportunity for growth, and he was going to be fairly compensated? This is why the Four Fundamentals of Employee Engagement are so important to our business; it is the promise that we make to our employees, and more often than not, it is the reason they choose to believe in us.

Because let me tell you, if somebody came to me with something that I felt like was going to change my life and create a great opportunity for me to grow, and I was going to make a ton of money, and all these things, I'm going. There is not going to be anything that stops me from going. If my girlfriend is uncertain, I'm going to sell her on the idea. And selling somebody on the idea of a business is, at the end of the day, the same way you sell a product. It's hard to go in and sell something if you can't articulate how it's going to make that person's life better. You have to start by stepping back and asking, "Is what I'm selling worth buying?" And if the answer is no, how can you change that? Because here's a secret: It's hard to go in and sell something you don't believe in.

CHAPTER 2

FISH IN A BIGGER POND

Hiring talent takes strategy, the same as selling a product. And yet so many companies leave their hiring practices up to chance. They wait to see who walks through their door and are disappointed when it isn't someone they want. In its most literal form, fishing in a bigger pond is about increasing the body of talent from which you are hiring. But it is also about being more strategic in your methods, being accountable when you fall short, and creating an environment that appeals to the kind of talent you wish to attract.

Your company is a reflection of yourself; if you are not attracting the talent you want, ask yourself what you have done or not done to create this outcome. Identify what it is you love about your company so you can sell the vision to prospective hires and develop a strategy to make sure your company is appealing to the ideal candidate. I don't believe that today's workforce is any less talented or hardworking than the workforces of generations past. If you are having trouble finding them, you likely are not looking in the right place.

FIX YOU FIRST

In the last chapters of the book *Start With Why*, Simon Sinek shares a story about how an archer shoots an arrow. In order to properly shoot an arrow, the archer has to pull the arrow back 180 degrees. I think this is a great image and really captures my business philosophy.

I believe that everything in business, and virtually everything in life, comes down to fixing yourself first. In order to fix yourself first in any situation, you have to step back and reflect. Ask yourself, "What could I have done differently in order to cause a different outcome?" It could be anything. If it's work-related, it could be how you process a title, or how

> *I believe that everything in business, and virtually everything in life, comes down to fixing yourself first.*

you process rebates. It could be how you communicate with other departments. It could be reflecting back on a situation where a customer came but you didn't get them to purchase something, or you weren't able to find a solution for them.

I want you to think of a couple of these scenarios where you could have done something differently and emerged with a different outcome. In order to do that, you have to take that step back; you cannot fix yourself until you fully understand what you did or did not do that led to the outcome you are currently facing.

I think the metaphor of shooting an arrow fits this idea perfectly. In order to shoot the arrow forward, you have to pull back. Simon Sinek uses it as an example of how every great advancement we have made in this country, in whatever the field, begins with pulling back. As individuals, I think it is so important we take the time to reflect and look back. If we look at every situation and identify what we could have done to create the best possible outcome, we allow ourselves the opportunity to reach that outcome in the future. We correct course and can fix problems because we know exactly where we went wrong.

If you're going to do well in business, if you're going to attract quality people, if you're going to sell at a high volume, if you're going to serve at a high volume, it starts with fixing you first. It's important when you're attracting and hiring talent that you look within first. If I didn't hire the last person I interviewed, why not? If it was a quality candidate, why weren't they hired? If it was not a quality candidate, what did I do to attract someone like this to my business?

My mindset as the leader of my organization is that 95% of what happens is because of something I did or did not do. As a manager, the more you hold yourself accountable to this practice, the more meaningful changes you are able to make. To start, ask, "Okay, I realize things are going to happen, but did I step up when they happened?" Then you can achieve an understanding of how to prevent that situation from happening in the future.

I have a responsibility to make people better, so if the wrong person is hired, or someone leaves out of the blue, that comes back to me. If an employee is not adhering to our core values, I need to hold myself accountable as much as I hold them accountable. I need to help them be a better person. In every instance, I will stop the bus to fix a problem because if I don't, I am not being a responsible leader.

In moments where you don't take the initiative to do the right thing, problems start to happen. When you see someone doing something that you know is not in their best interest, and you allow it to happen, that is you failing as a manager. That is not caring for your employees, it's just not. When I have those conversations, I have them not from a place of anger, but a place of care. I care about this person, and I need them to do the right thing.

I see my daughter doing it now too. I've watched her take people twice her age and call them out point blank, saying, "You cannot do that here. You cannot act that way." Even for minor infractions. She says, "This is what great looks like, and this is what we're going to do. If you can't, this may not be the right place for you." And the amazing thing is her employees aren't quitting; they are staying longer because of it. They can tell she really cares about them and holds them to the same standard she holds herself to. They would say, "At my other job, they just let me go, or they ignored me or shut me out." They know now they are part of a team, and they love her for it.

This process of accountability goes both ways. It is not just me stepping in when I see an employee doing something wrong. It also means my employees have the ability to communicate and be heard when they feel something needs to change. We have a practice called a 555 in which the employee evaluates their relationship with you as a leader. We do this evaluation quarterly and ask our employees to answer the Four Fundamentals, as well as questions like:

- How well do you feel management communicates with you?
- Do you feel you are part of the team?
- List one thing you feel that if we changed or altered would significantly impact our business.

What we are trying to accomplish by asking these questions is prompt them to give us feedback that leads to opportunities to grow our relationship. These questions all ultimately reflect back on me. I am everyone's manager. Hopefully, I can uncover methods to improve my own communication and my own relationship with our employees.

If someone answers that they only sometimes feel like part of the team, that alerts me that there is an issue there and prompts me to investigate it. I want to have a conversation with that individual and get to the bottom of it, and I need to do it as quickly as possible. In these situations, the sooner you act, the less infected the wound becomes. There is a reason that the employee wrote that. They want to feel like a member of the team all of the time and want us to know that is not where they are at right now. More likely than not, it is something I am doing or not doing that is causing this person to feel that way. It may be that I made a joke about someone in a meeting, or I didn't give them enough of my time. What you are trying to do in this practice is gather information and correct any problems as quickly as possible. Because there is always something you can do that causes a different outcome.

We also do an exercise where employees are asked to name three people that would allow them to dominate the industry. I do this exercise all the time. I get that feedback because it tells me where an employee is at mentally. If someone is not listing their direct supervisor as someone who could help them dominate the industry, there is probably an issue there. It means their supervisor is not impacting their life in a profound and positive way. And it may sound cheesy, but that is what we want all our employees to feel: inspired and impacted.

I then ask my employees the last two people they would take to dominate the industry. It doesn't mean they wouldn't take them, but they would be the employee's last choice. Lo and behold, if a supervisor doesn't show up on the first list, they almost certainly will show up on the second. If an employee doesn't feel like they are a part of the team, they don't feel their supervisors are communicating with them, it is my job to get to the bottom of it. And it is the employee's job to communicate to me how I can help them.

Another purpose of asking these questions is to empower my employees to share how they truly feel. They need to know they can give constructive feedback without being reprimanded or ignored. Far too often, when things go wrong with an employee, managers will say, "I didn't know! They never told me," without ever considering what they might have done to cause the employee to feel they could not share their concerns.

I need my employees to know that I too have skin in this game. Weak managers will push an issue aside and not address it, but I know the reason that this employee feels the way he does can be traced back to something I did or did not do. A lot of leaders don't want to trace the problem back to themselves, but I do because it means the solution to the problem is within my power. If my actions caused a problem, my actions could fix it too. We practice this at every level of the business. People are quick to point a finger at someone else, but if everyone can fix themselves first, the entire company benefits.

SOMETHING GOOD OUT OF LOSS

I have a friend of mine who also runs his own company. He has been running it for a long time. Recently, his right-hand person turned in their resignation, and it was a complete surprise. If you had asked him who was least likely to leave, he would have said this person. We were talking about it, and I told him, "Obviously, it is your fault. Let's call a spade a spade. Something happened that made this person leave, so let's try to make a good thing out of your loss."

I told him to take out a piece of paper and draw a line down the middle. On one side he wrote all of the things he absolutely loved about this person, all the things that make them impossible to replace. On the other side he wrote down all the skills and attributes he wished this person could have done better at or had more of.

This exercise is important because when you have had someone with you for a long time, you become dependent on them, you trust them. And if they all of a sudden leave, there is a hole. But you have also realized in your heart that there was something going on, and you were ignoring it, both on a personal and business level. Unless there is absolutely nothing this person could have improved upon, it is likely that you as their superior weren't pushing them to be their best, and that could have contributed to their leaving. Now, this exercise is not an opportunity to bash an employee for leaving. But when you take the time to really reflect, those things come to the surface.

It has to be a diligent and measurable action. Don't just make a mental checklist, actually write it down. If you only do it in your head, there is no accountability. It is much more difficult to reflect and make sure you actually lived up to the expectations you set for yourself. But if you write it down, you can look back at that list when you are hiring and choose the candidate who is best equipped to fulfill both sides of the list.

My friend called me a few days later and said, "John. That conversation changed my perspective. I was sitting here thinking we would never be able to replace the person because they were so fantastic, but seeing there was room for improvement helped me realize what I have to do."

This is how you turn a loss into something good. By tracing the problem back to you, figuring out what you could have done differently, you are actively learning and benefiting from the situation.

Now, I'm not going to say that I have never lost somebody by surprise, because I'm sure I have. But it has become rare because I try to stay close to my people. I try to understand where their head and heart are at, and if they are thinking of leaving, hopefully I can impact that decision. And if it does happen, if someone does leave, you can be sure I'm going to go back in and figure out what happened. If I can put aside my ego and recognize what I personally could have done differently, things will recover. There might be a jolt, it might even be devastating, but if I as an individual can be better for it, my company will too.

> *By tracing the problem back to you, figuring out what you could have done differently, you are actively learning and benefiting from the situation.*

A message I will repeat over and over in this book is that understanding and identifying what great looks like will attract great into your life. You want to be great for all of your employees. If one of your employees is leaving, you still want to be great for them. You want to celebrate their opportunity, not react negatively. But then you have to assess the situation, and if the new job is better for that person, you should celebrate that this job created a valuable opportunity for them, and then consider how you can make this position even better for the next person.

When you lose a valued employee, you need to focus on how you can trade up. The only way you can trade up is by knowing what trading looks like. I can't tell you how many times I have seen business managers, both in my company and in others, settle for the next employee that comes along. They assume that the next employee is going to be equal to the one they had before, but in truth, they are often less because those hiring are so desperate to fill that position.

In that situation, the most important thing you can do is immediately identify what was really happening in that situation. Identify what the person did well and what they could have done better. When you go through a breakup, the first thing you see is all the good times. Your memory works in such a way that you only see the positive things you are missing out on. But the quicker you can get past that and get to the reality of the situation, the quicker you can identify what qualities you are going to gain in your new hire. If you are only thinking, "Oh, so and so was so great at this and that," you won't see the opportunity to trade up, to get an even better employee.

Earl Nightingale says, "What the mind sees and believes can be achieved." You have to have a clear image of what you want before you can make it a reality, and you have to believe in it. Most people don't know what they are looking for, let alone believe in it. They only see what they are losing or missing and are not looking for the opportunity for something better.

When an employee leaves, and you are unable to look at the situation honestly and with clarity, you are actively limiting the size of the pond you are fishing in. Fishing in a bigger pond means having access to the widest possible range of prospective hires, so you can find the individual best suited for the job. But when you hold prospective hires to an unrealistic image of the previous employee or hire out of a desperate need to fill that position, you are limiting your opportunity to find the perfect fit. You are going against what great looks like for that position.

LOVE WHAT YOU DO

When hiring, you have to ask yourself: Do I believe in this vision? Do I believe in this business model? Is it strong enough that when someone sits in front of me, I can convince them without any restrictions whatsoever? The answer to all of those questions needs to be "yes" if prospective employees are going to be willing to forgo the big income that they could possibly get elsewhere. But they will be willing to do that if they believe in you, and if they believe in your vision and their place in it.

If I am working my way up from the bottom and trying to go after attracting people on a shoestring budget, that's how I would do it. I'm not going to sell somebody something that I don't believe in myself; it starts with me. And even now that I can afford to offer good salaries to my employees, I still won't sell them on a vision if I don't fully believe in it myself.

I'll give you a good example. About 20 years ago, I was having doubts about whether I was doing exactly what I wanted to do. One of my really close friends had a closed-circuit television business. He was making really good money, he wasn't working nearly as many hours as I was, and overall, he was killing it. He tried to convince me to go into his business.

For two days I went and rode with him in his business circuit to see if his career appealed to me. I trusted that it would because we were totally like-minded individuals, both students of leadership books, educated in similar ways, and our businesses were very similar. We both had service, we both had sales, and we both had parts. There were a lot of crossovers; selling is consistent in some ways regardless of the product. It's building relationships with people and gaining trust.

He had three accounts that day, so we got up in the morning and we drove about an hour and a half to the first one. We met with some business owners, and he did his presentation. He went through his presentation but didn't close the deal, so we left and headed to the next one. We drove another hour and a half to the second location, and at this point it was lunchtime, so we ate lunch before we went in because those folks had a 1:30 appointment.

Finally, we go meet with them, and we sit in the waiting room for half an hour. They eventually come out, and he does his presentation, then we get on to the next one. I did this a couple of times, and as glamorous as his business looked on the outside, I realized I was taking for granted what I did every day. That was the first time I ever really realized how much I love what I do.

After these appointments, we went back to his place and played foosball in his garage. Mid-play, he stopped and said, "You didn't like it."

"What are you talking about?" I said.

"No, you didn't like my business."

"No, no, it was great," I said. "Stop, let's play."

He said, "No, I'm not playing 'til you tell me what it is that you didn't like about it."

Finally, I said, "You know, it's not what I didn't like about it. It's that I realized I love what I do. I work in a building with 50, 60 people that all have lives, they have problems, and they have successes, and they have kids who are graduating school, kids who are getting in trouble, and kids who are getting married, or they're breaking up. But I'm in their lives, and I realized that I love that. And I love to walk into the store and see a customer of mine that I helped with their family vehicle. Because I deal straight, and I do what I say I'm going to do, I don't have to hide. I could hold my head high and know that I did everything I could to serve them and become a part of the community."

Until that time, I did not realize how much I love every minute of that. Now I can't imagine being in a job where I don't get to do that. So, when you talk about attracting employees, you have to be able to share with them why you do what you do. When you are able to successfully articulate this, they feel your passion, and they see your purpose. When people can see your plan, they can't help but hook their cart to your train. They just have to, because maybe their life can be like your life, or maybe they can find the joy in what it is that they do in the same way you do.

> **If you're going to attract people, you better have something attractive to show them. It starts with you.**

If you're going to attract people, you better have something attractive to show them. It starts with you. It starts with you believing in what it is you're doing, and your belief is so strong that people get caught up in the wave and have no choice but to join forces with you. Now, keeping them is a whole different thing, but we will get there.

IDENTIFY THE POND

Recently, we've been experiencing a lot of growth in our company, and because of that, a new vacancy opened up. We now had a need for two different positions, one in accounting and one in service. A conversation emerged because we had begun the recruitment process, but we weren't having any success. Unemployment is at an all-time high; there are more jobs than ever but nobody to fill them. We said, "Okay, let's take a step back and pretend we're scouring the job market looking for a position as a title clerk or a similar opportunity." We tried to get ourselves in the mindset of someone who would ideally be applying for our position. We began thinking about this, and we wondered, if a prospective employee is moving to our area, they're doing an internet search, how are they going to find our company?

We did the search ourselves and interestingly enough, we didn't come up on any of the job search engines. We were using Indeed at the time, as that's one of our primary spots through which we list our job opportunities. We pretended we were a random person, and we typed in "title clerk." We began with a big search throughout the state of North Carolina, so we weren't too surprised when we didn't show up there.

We narrowed it down to the counties we operate in, and our listing didn't show up there either. We went even smaller to the cities we work in, and none of our listings showed up. And the reason this was so concerning is because we actively pay for our job positions to be listed on Indeed. We discovered that unless you do a targeted campaign and refresh the page constantly, our listing didn't show up until you get to the 15th or 20th page, despite the fact that we were paying them to have our job listings seen. If you were a person looking for either of the opportunities we had available, you would never be able to find us.

When you're fishing for personnel for your company, whatever your company is, all of the steps you are taking to attract talent won't matter if your voice isn't being heard. It doesn't matter how long you stand on the dock, if your bait isn't in the water, you're not really fishing, you're just holding the pole. The same principle applies to recruiting. The only way you will be able to hire who you want is if you have the opportunity to interview who you want. It was a stark moment of realization. Everything I just discussed about fixing you first and selling your vision - that attitude is so dear to my philosophy, and it still stands, but it isn't going to matter if nobody is seeing my advertisements in the first place.

> *It doesn't matter how long you stand on the dock, if your bait isn't in the water, you're not really fishing, you're just holding the pole. The same principle applies to recruiting.*

In the hiring process, there are so many small elements to manage and pay attention to, that it can be easy to miss something big. If you are so focused on using the right bait, getting the perfect hook, and finding a nice spot where you are sure to catch all of the fish, you are less likely to notice that your line wasn't in the water the whole time. This is when I like to use the exercise of thinking about my company and position from the perspective of a potential hire.

Where might a prospective hire see ads for my company? What do those ads say about us? What comes up when they search my company's name on the internet? How are we regarded in the community? If they ask their friends and family about my company, what are they likely to hear? If you are having trouble hiring quality candidates, trace the process back to the potential hire and where they may or may not be receiving the necessary information. Identify the pond you are fishing in, and if something is stopping the process, adjust. It may be as simple as your bait not being fully in the water.

NOT ALL PONDS ARE EQUAL

Keeping up with the pond analogy, it is also worth noting that not all ponds are inherently equal. Not all ponds are going to yield the same caliber of fish. For a long time, there was a very specific type of person who applied for our sales jobs, and they were truthfully not the kind of employees we wanted. These were people who were lost. They didn't know what to do in their lives, or they had failed at whatever their previous job had been, and so they thought,

"Well, I'll try sales." For some reason, the pond we were fishing in was yielding people who weren't sure what they wanted to do with their lives and more than likely hadn't succeeded in their past jobs, otherwise, they would still be doing whatever they had been doing before.

We realized this was a small pond, and we were limiting ourselves by only fishing in that pond. We began thinking about how our businesses operate in an area surrounded by seven major universities; there is a big potential workforce that we had been leaving untapped. These kids are graduating year in and year out with business and marketing degrees, and they might not know the exact place they want to work, but they know what they want to do. We can also assume, generally, that they are going to meet some of our criteria. We know that they are career-minded because they have invested in their education. We know that they're pretty smart because they were able to get through college and graduate. But these kids are going to work for Enterprise, Verizon, Apple, companies that don't provide the benefits, work environment, and quality of life that we do.

How do we put ourselves in a position where we can fish for those applicants as well as the applicants we're already getting? I'm not saying that what we were already getting was bad, but on its own, it wasn't ideal. We were trying to broaden our reach. Because if we can attract recent grads, we broaden our pool of candidates from 100 people to thousands. So instead of trying to find the one gem in 100, we're trying to find many gems in a pool of hundreds of thousands.

CHAPTER 3

USE THE RIGHT BAIT

No matter how small your business is, no matter how restricted you are in your hiring practices, there are people out there who are doing the job or a job similar to yours. The issue is not that the talent doesn't exist, you simply haven't attracted them. You aren't fishing with the right bait. That bait has to motivate a feeling inside the candidate that what you do and what you have is going to bring value into their life in some way.

In advertising, we teach the principle of greed and larceny. Greed means that the product or service offers so much to the customer that they have to do business with you. Larceny means the product or service is so affordable, is of such value, that the customer can't pass up the opportunity. Now, these terms have a negative connotation, but in their simplest form, they mean motivating the customer to do something other than what they originally planned.

When you are trying to hire someone, it is the same principle. The bait needs to fulfill those desires. Either they are going to get so much education and opportunity out of this position they can't help but take it, or they are going to make so much money from working for you that it would be a loss not to. You cannot attract quality employees without bait that appeals to their specific needs.

REMOVE BARRIERS TO ENTRY

Returning to the topic of hiring recent college graduates, we began this mission by asking our interns a few questions: What are your generation's barriers of entry to working here? What is it that your generation, your educated class, wants in a career coming out of college? By taking the time to ask multiple people of that demographic, we were able to identify what those things were, and more so, we realized we already had those qualities, we just weren't representing it in a way that was attractive to this specific audience. For example, one of the barriers to entry was uncertainty of pay.

When a student would come in for an interview, the manager would tell them, "If you're really good, you'll make between X and Y."

And the students would ask, "What pay can you guarantee?"

"We can guarantee minimum wage." Now the students go home and tell their parents who just paid 100 grand on education that they are only going to be making minimum wage.

Naturally, Mom and Dad are going to look at them and say, "No way. Don't go work there. Are you crazy?"

We figured out a way to make a pay ladder that did exactly what a commission would do, except it was guaranteed. We were able to provide certainty where before there had been doubt. Now we say, "Okay, if you come in at this level, do your training for 90 days, you move to this level. If you meet certain metrics you can graduate to the next level, which receives this income. These metrics have nothing to do with how much you sell, it has to do with how many presentations you do." This proved to be really exciting for potential hires because they could not only see exactly how much money they would make upon being hired, but they had clear metrics and requirements for how they would progress in the future.

The second big barrier to entry was a fear of one-on-one negotiations. Because of the internet, pricing has been consistently established across the board. The need for negotiations is a lot smaller. We had known this for a long time, but we didn't know that it was a source of anxiety for prospective hires. Once we knew that, we could emphasize right off the bat that they wouldn't have to do much negotiating with customers. We could tell them, "When it gets to the point of talking about the financials, we'll have a manager do that." This took a lot of the weight off our salespeople; all they have to do is build a relationship with that customer, which most people want to do anyway.

Another barrier of entry was the stigma of the car salesman position. People have a stereotype in mind of car salesmen as greasy scam artists. Now, we know that's just a stereotype, but if we can remove a barrier to entry, we will. We really emphasized the position wasn't a car salesman, it was a product specialist. We have car salesmen whose pay is based on commission; this position is not that. This position is a product specialist, and your job is to present the product and build a relationship with the customer. We knew from our data that for every four customers our product specialists talk to, they make one sale. We emphasized this and let our new hires know we're not grading them on sales, we're grading them on what produces the sales. Not having to focus on closing a sale freed our employees up to relax and really focus on the customer, and that care and attention they naturally gave are what we grade them on. Grading them on what happens organically gives them the freedom to become excellent at their jobs.

Once you have identified the barriers to entry and figured out how to remedy them, the next step is to decide how to get this information to the masses. We sat down as a group, and we decided to go straight to the placement officers at the universities. Their job is to get their students employed so the university can keep saying, "Our school places 83% of our graduates." These people have an obligation to find placement for their students; it is in both of our best interests to work together. Instead of solely running ads on Indeed or doing commercials, we started going to job fairs and to the universities and saying, "Here is our program. Here is what it does. This is the pay that you will be guaranteed. This is the education you'll receive." We put all that information into a pamphlet, gave it to the placement officers, and they did the recruiting for us.

When I say you have to use the right bait, what I mean in its purest form is to take the job you have, identify what the ideal candidate for that job looks like, and make the job attractive to them. This can involve what we did, removing existing barriers to entry so that our ideal employee has no hang-ups about the position, or it could mean further incentivizing an already great position. Think about your ideal employee. What might this person need in order to make a position so appealing they can't possibly say no? Now make it a reality.

> *Take the job you have, identify what the ideal candidate for that job looks like, and make the job attractive to them.*

DIFFERENT BAIT FOR DIFFERENT PEOPLE

The only way to make sure you are fishing with the right bait is by listening to your people. You have to know what people want. A while back, I was watching the House voting on a bill not to tax PPP funds. I was listening to the speakers, many of whom were small-business owners. This one woman came out and she immediately started talking about how her restaurant had a million dollars' worth of sales. I could tell right away that she had lost a large percentage of her audience. Any good salesman knows you cater your content to your audience. As soon as she said that, the audience saw her as some rich lady trying to keep her wealth, as opposed to a business owner they can ally with. I thought, "Man, she is not using the right bait." She didn't understand that what she was saying was actually the opposite of what her audience wanted to hear.

When it comes to using the right bait, you have to use the right bait for the fish you're trying to catch. Different people are going to want different things out of a job, and it's not always about the money. When you are recruiting new talent, you need to be prepared to meet a variety of needs. Those needs may be time off, it may be about benefits. What works for recent college grads is not going to work for someone who has been in the workforce for 30 years. There is also the simple fact that candidates will feel more comfortable if the person hiring them is of like mind; they will be more confident that this person understands their needs. Whoever you are trying to hire should also be the one doing the hiring.

> ***Whoever you are trying to hire should also be the one doing the hiring.***

You have to figure out what motivates the type of person you are trying to attract. I use this analogy because fishermen understand this: You go to any tackle store in the country, and you see a wall of different baits, and that's because different fish like different things. It's no different with humanity. Your desires in a career vary depending on the stage of life you are in. For a young professional, having a ladder to success is crucial because they are just now starting to build their career. For someone who is 50 and married with kids, they are going to want benefits that extend to their family and the security to keep them provided for until they retire. They still need a ladder, but it may be less of a motivator than the benefits. If the bait you're using to attract talent isn't working, switch baits.

Providing the right bait does not end when you hire an employee. Our Four Fundamentals are designed in such a way that if an employee can answer yes to all four, we know we are continuing to provide the right bait for that person. For example, if an employee affirms that yes, they are growing, we can assume that there is a ladder in place for their success. Therefore, we make a point to continually readdress the Four Fundamentals at our quarterly meetings.

Sometimes it will become apparent that we have a store or department where a significant number of employees no longer feel they can answer yes to the first three questions. Their pay hasn't changed, they are still being fairly compensated, but the first three may have slipped.

- **Does what I do matter?**
- **Do I have a voice?**
- **Am I growing?**

These concepts are a bit more abstract and therefore harder to maintain. We needed to discover why this was happening. One thing we do is look at trends. A good example is that years ago in our sales department, everyone had a five-day work week except for the last week of the month. The last week of the month we have everybody on, and nobody takes a day off. We didn't invent this idea; it was just part of the industry at that time. And while I'm sure people weren't happy about it back in the day, nobody said anything. It was widely understood that this was just the way it was.

The younger generation coming in was different. They were more aware of their time. It wasn't that they were lazy, but they came of age in a period where the lines of work-life balance were drawn a lot more clearly than they were for my generation. For people straight out of college, they're still working 8, 10, 12 hours a day, but they also want their time.

I constantly give my employees surveys and ask them questions to gauge where their head is at—I will discuss this more at length later. But one of the questions I ask them is, "If you could change one thing about this business, what would it be?" And the most common answer I received was time. They wanted more time of their own to spend with their family and friends.

We sat down and we talked it over as a group, and we decided that it actually didn't make sense to have people work the entire last week of the month. And the reason why was because it actually ended up taking away productivity for the first week of the following month. By the following week, everyone was so burnt out that the time they worked didn't actually end up boosting our sales or productivity in any way. We voted to no longer have employees work for the full seven days the last week of the month.

We also voted on what we could do to generally improve the workplace, and one thing that came up was spending more time together outside of work. We would have company picnics where everyone's families came and got involved. But we wanted to do more of that. We don't want our employees to feel like we are taking them away from their families, but to feel like we are a part of their family. We put someone in charge of planning an annual Easter Day. We got cornhole contests, we rented bouncy houses for the little kids, and we sponsored a farmer's market and a corn maze. It turned out great; they actually cut the corn maze into our logo so you could see our logo from an aerial view. We invited the whole company and all their families, so in total there were 600–700 people there.

Now, I want to make an important note. When I tell this story, I often hear people my age complain about the younger demographic, or I will hear people in the industry complain about how they struggle to hire millennials. I am always quick to debunk that idea. I admire the younger people in my company for advocating for themselves and letting us know that they needed more time; the whole company benefited from them because of it. I'm of the opinion that the younger generation can resource data so much faster than any previous generation. They can efficiently maneuver through such a wide variety of tasks. It's amazing. What I find is that when people talk about lazy millennials, they are only looking at a few people. They're not looking at the career-minded young people the way we did. I've gotten pushback from people in my industry who say that they can't get millennials to work. I say you're still looking at the 100 people who can't find a job and don't know what they really want to be doing, you're not going after the hundreds of thousands that are trying to build a career.

You may be struggling with lazy young people, but there were plenty of lazy people in my generation too, and the generation prior, and the generation before them. I've noticed it since I was a kid; every generation thinks the one after them is inferior. My parents' generation certainly felt that way about mine. No matter the generation, if you seek out negativity, you will find it. If you seek out positive, hard-working individuals, you will find them too.

I am always trying to identify the things that are the most important to our employees. How can we impact change right now? And time off was a big one. So even though removing the seven-day work week made sense economically, I would have done it anyway because it was for the well-being of our employees, so they could keep answering yes to the Four Fundamentals.

If you stop providing the right bait for your employees the moment you hire them, you are almost guaranteed to lose them down the line. As I said earlier, I want my employees to be motivated to stay with us for the entirety of their careers. That means continually assessing what the right bait looks like as they grow within the company. Meeting the needs of your employees is not a one-off decision, and it is never stagnant. It means continually assessing what makes a position desirable and implementing those factors.

KEEP THE FLAME LIT

A lot of companies these days strive to burn through employees, particularly young ones. They work their employees to the bone and let them go because, in their eyes, they have an unending labor supply. People don't stop getting older, right? You see this all the time. People will enter a program on fire, they go through the training on fire, and they begin work in the position on fire. But over time, the flame starts dwindling, and before you know it, the flame is out. And nobody minds because this is exactly what they expected.

That is not how I do business, and ultimately, that is why I don't struggle with hiring. I always say, "When I hire people, I hire 'em forever." It means that my intention when you come to work for this company is that you never want to leave. And ultimately, that desire to stay is based on trust, because if you don't trust me, then you will likely leave. If I'm selling you on a vision and a program, everybody needs to deliver on that program. And the only way you can get people to deliver on a program is if they've also bought into it and they also understand its purpose. It takes the entire company believing in your vision to live up to the promise you make to prospective hires. And in doing so, we continue to live up to the promise I made to my current hires, the people I hired before them, and so on and so forth.

That's also why as a company, we continue to expand. I'm at a place in my life where I don't have to worry about money. You ask yourself, why should I put myself out there, why take a chance and buy more stores? But as you develop, people grow within your organization. I see it as my obligation to create opportunities for them, and the only way to do that is to get bigger. My goal has never been to expand my company for the sake of money. I have always grown because my employees have, and I want to match them step for step. If my employees are growing and my company is not, they will inevitably reach a point where they can no longer answer yes to that third fundamental: Am I growing?

> **I have always grown because my employees have, and I want to match them step for step.**

I also believe in my heart that you're either green and growing, or you're ripe and rotting. You need to make sure that you're constantly trying to push yourself to become more and better, bigger, faster, and stronger. I do that in every aspect of my life. A few years ago, I bought a plane and learned how to fly it. And as much as I enjoy planes, it's not a matter of luxury. It's because I am constantly traveling to speaking engagements and learning how to fly a plane was something that I knew would make me better as a person and was cost efficient. I'm constantly evaluating the situation and asking, "How can we make it better?" For both myself and my employees. "How can I give them new opportunities? How can I ensure they are getting to the next level in their knowledge and skills?" The answer is to continue expanding. But expanding looks different for every business.

What can you do to keep empowering your employees to grow? How can you keep the flame lit?

CREATE A LADDER

You can't keep someone forever without a plan to elevate them. If I want my employees to want to stay, if I am going to uphold the commitment I made to them upon hiring, I need to ensure there is a ladder in place for their success.

It is difficult to work without a secure knowledge of how your career is going to advance because of the work you are doing now. Think about it. When kids are in elementary school, it's all about next year. They know if they get good grades, they'll pass first grade, and they get to go to the second grade. And then if they get good grades, they get to go to the third grade and so on. Your whole life you think about high school, and you know if you get good grades in high school it will create an opportunity for you in college. You are conditioned from the time you are a child to prepare for the next step, but if you don't know what that next step is, you lose the motivation to perform well. You spend 12–16 years in an incredibly linear system, and then you enter the working world, and they just stick you in a job. You work a job day-to-day not knowing what's next, not knowing where that ladder leads. It can be incredibly frustrating.

When we designed our product specialist program, one of the big things we concentrated on was the mindset of recent college graduates. Recent grads are always wanting to do more in the world. They want a raise, they want more money, they want more opportunity, whatever it may be. That is why we put a ladder in place. For the first 90 days they are in this specific program, and after those 90 days they qualify for the next program, and after a certain amount of time, and they meet certain requirements, they qualify for the next one.

College graduates are used to a structured environment because their life has been a constant series of steps and levels. We wanted to recreate that structure in our workplace so that they aren't thinking about their next job elsewhere, they're thinking about moving up to the next level in our company.

There are three things that I think anyone should know when leading recent college graduates trying to find their place in the world. First, you have got to make sure they understand the Peak to Peek principle. The Peak to Peek principle by Dr. Robert Schuller explains that you can't see your next peak until you climb the mountain in front of you. You can't see your next accomplishment until you complete your immediate goals. And while this principle is often true in life, I want my employees to be able to see the next peak from miles away. At any job, there are going to be things you like, and there are going to be things you dislike. But those challenges become easier to manage if you can see where you are going, and if you get used to winning all the time, you find that the next peak becomes closer and closer.

The best thing young people can do at this stage of their life is become a winner. How do you become a winner? Win where you're at. Win where you're at so that when you move to whatever comes next, you're

> *At any job, there are going to be things you like, and there are going to be things you dislike. But those challenges become easier to manage if you can see where you are going.*

doing it to better yourself and not running from what you've got. I think that's an important piece a lot of people in business overlook.

I always make sure my employees can see the ladder. I make sure they know how to win where they're at, and that they can see what the next peak looks like within our company. When I first started working on this seven or eight years ago, I was actually surprised because developing a ladder for each position was much easier than I had originally thought. I was thinking, "How do you set up a ladder upfront so someone can see it when you're trying to draw them into your business?" And what felt really daunting was actually quite simple.

To develop the future of a position, you have to

understand the future of your business. What does your company look like in 3 years, in 5 years, in 10 years? Are you bigger? How are roles and responsibilities going to change the larger you get? By taking what you have now and multiplying out those positions by the number that would be needed when you get to that size, the gaps and needs create themselves. When you try to plan your own future, if you're doing your job right, that vision also impacts the futures of your employees, and you need to account for them in that vision as well.

I find this to be a helpful exercise. Think about your business now. Think about your current staff, their size, what each specific role is, and what it takes to manage them. Imagine the ideal size you would like to have in five years. Are there positions that can be done by one person, or are you going to need more people as your success grows? Are those new people going to need someone to report to? Could the person who is filling that role now grow to show others how to do it? You have a miniature ladder for growth right there.

THROW THE STICK

I have discussed this story in my previous book, *Why Jacob Matters*, but I find it to be relevant here as well. Several years ago, my son-in-law was working in banking and experiencing much of the same uncertainties I explained earlier. He did not have a clear path forward or an understanding of where opportunity for growth was going to be in the future. One day he shared his thoughts with me: "I'm not sure what direction the bank wants me to go, and I'm not sure the options are what I want for my future," he said.

There are many different directions you can go into in the banking industry: loans, investments, and so on. But in that instance, there was no path laid out for him in which he could see the future and feel good about it.

I told him the same story I tell everyone who asks me for advice in this kind of situation.

"Listen," I said. "I read a story in a book one time, and it was talking about a bunch of people that were hired to pick a huge thousand-acre cornfield. The farmer told them, 'Okay, you've got to pick all this corn by the end of the week.'

"And the workers were looking around at how many of them there were, and they're saying, 'There's no way we're going to pick this field. This is crazy.' But one of the workers was a natural leader, and he knew all the other workers and had their trust.

"He says, 'Hey. Listen, guys. We're sitting here complaining about having to pick this whole field, and we're not getting anything done. And yeah, we probably won't get it all picked, but let's throw a stick as far as we can throw it, and let's just pick until we reach that stick. Once we get to that stick, we'll make a decision. We'll either throw it again, or we'll stop.' They go ahead and reach the stick and decide to throw it again, and again, and again, until lo and behold, they pick the whole field."

My point to my son-in-law in telling him this was, "You're undecided, but when people are undecided, they don't accomplish anything. They spend their time looking for what's wrong or what's right about what they're doing and believe me, they find both. You're at a crossroads, and you're not sure what decision to make, so you need to throw a stick.

"You need to set a date and say, 'You know what, I'm going to keep my head down, and I'm going to do the very best that I can until this date. And then I'm either going to choose to pick up my stick, go home and head in a different direction, or I'm going to throw that stick again.' But the exercise is to keep your head down, concentrate, and give it your all, even if it's not doing something you love. In my experience, when you do that, the opportunity comes to you, either for growth in your current field, or a new opportunity in a different field."

A guy said this to me a long time ago: "John, once you get good at running, you never get good at anything else," he said. "Win at what you're doing and then the next thing will become evident to you."

I believe in winning where you're at. There is always going to be something shiny that draws the eye, but if you understand the way your current work contributes to your long-term goal, even if it is only to prove to yourself that you are ready for a change, you can win where you are at while being secure in the fact that you are working towards your long-term goal.

If you think about the way a mountain is shaped, it's wide at the base, and it's narrow at the top. The theory is that the higher you climb, the farther you can see. Whatever mountain you're on right now, climb it as high as you can, and your next move will become clear to you. I have always tried to live my life that way.

> **Whatever mountain you're on right now, climb it as high as you can, and your next move will become clear to you.**

My son-in-law took my advice. He gave himself a time frame and dedicated that time to giving his all to the job, really committing himself to it. His hard work paid off; during that time, he entered a new position at the bank and began to work on the Hiester Automotive account we had with the bank. Some issues emerged that required my son-in-law to work closely with the controller at our company and become involved in our business.

The great thing that happens when people stick their heads down and become great at what they're doing, is that the path forward becomes clear. When people focus on doing their very best at their jobs, not only do they become better at what they do, but opportunities come to them, and they can identify a path forward where before there were none.

My son-in-law focused on winning where he was at and because of that effort, he received the opportunity to work on our accounts. Through that opportunity, he spent time with our controller and learned a lot from her; he felt like this was a chance to not only make a difference in our company, but to grow and learn from her. He approached me one day and shared that in our dealings with the bank, he was feeling like he was on the wrong side of it. He wanted to work on our side of the table and be a part of our company. He left the bank on an incredibly positive note. Where before he had been confused and unclear, he now saw a path forward.

I don't want employees who are going to run at the first sign of uncertainty. If you are going to leave a job, you should do it because you are confident in what you are moving towards, not because you are running from something else. I want employees who are going to throw the stick, who are going to try their hardest to win where they are at. But I also want to give them opportunities so that they don't have to constantly decide if they want to continue working for me. I want to give them everything they need to know that Hiester Automotive is where they want to be.

CHAPTER 4

EVERYONE MATTERS

When it comes to attracting talent, everyone matters. Therefore, you need to treat everyone with the same respect and attention you would a prized employee. What many businesses don't understand is that you need to sell your company to prospective hires the same way you would to customers. The best way you can make your company synonymous with quality positions, excellent customer service, and great work culture is by exhibiting these qualities to everyone you meet.

We make sure all of my employees have a ladder to success so that they will go out and share their victories with the people in their life, and in doing so, attract others to our company. I make sure I hire people who treat our vendors with the same goodwill and kindness they would customers. I make sure our customers feel welcomed and included to the point where they want to become employees.

Those vendors then speak highly of our businesses to everyone else they service. So much of this book is about loving people. I have discussed how loving people means accountability—and I will talk more about accountability in this chapter—but it also means treating everyone as if they matter.

I don't practice this just because it benefits my business, and I don't hire employees who behave this way because it will benefit them. I have always lived my life in accordance with these values, and I want my employees to do the same. Having it pay off in attracting, inspiring, and motivating talent is simply a happy accident.

EMPLOYEES ATTRACT EMPLOYEES

One thing that has been incredibly helpful to our organization is using our employees to attract talent. The best source of candidates within our organization is our employees. Now, this is often the first thing people think of when they are discussing attracting talent. They'll say, "Hey, let's throw a bonus out there for our employees if they'll bring somebody." But that's not really the point. The point is your employees have to love your business enough to want to help you fill those positions. Tricking them or giving them an incentive is not going to work if they don't really care about your business. I want my employees to care enough about the success of this business so that when they see a void, they're right beside me, they're thinking, "We need to fill that void. Who would be a good fit for our organization?" I want them to be talking to their peers and to their friends. And I want them to be networking with me to fill those positions.

I've found that in moments where people with skilled trades are in high demand and in short supply, I have more than enough. Why is that? It's simple. The people that want to work here, work here. When your employees are winning, they tell their friends, they tell their family, their friends and family tell other people, and before you know it, everyone wants to work for you.

I use IBM as an example because when I moved to North Carolina, IBM was one of the largest employers in the state. They had their research center here. And something I noticed was that everyone who worked for IBM was consistently proud of it. They didn't hide where they worked, they didn't say, "I'm in the IT field." They said, "I work for IBM." The reason for this was because IBM took care of their people. They communicated with them; they developed a method for their employees to understand their jobs. They had a tier system so different jobs fell into different levels. The employees understood that if they moved up in the levels, they would get paid more. They were constantly looking for opportunities to better the company so that they could better themselves. Many companies in the U.S. start out this way, but they end up losing the fundamental principle that employees are key to success and start focusing solely on the balance sheet instead. You lose this culture when you prioritize profit over people.

It was so powerful that their employees wanted to stay there forever. They all wore the same blue or white shirts. You could see them when you walked in a restaurant, and you knew, that's probably someone from IBM. They wore it proudly. It was a brand. So many companies lose that because they forget why they do what they do. It stops being about the people.

> **When you center your business around the success of your employees, your employees will ensure you have a successful business.**

I say in my business, "I'm creating a community of people who can contribute and give back because they're succeeding, they're winning, they're getting paid." My job is to make sure that I'm hiring people that can succeed within that framework, and that I'm holding them accountable to stay the course to be able to experience that level of happiness and victory in their careers. Because when you center your business around the success of your employees, your employees will ensure you have a successful business.

VENDORS ATTRACT EMPLOYEES

I think what separates us from other companies and why we struggle less with hiring is because people feel loved when they walk into our business. It's that simple. They feel it in the showroom, they feel it in the service department, they feel it in the parts department. They feel it in every single aspect of our company. The biggest salespeople we have for our company are honestly our vendors. I'm talking about the people that deliver from Staples, or fix the dents on our vehicles, or do maintenance work around our buildings. We have a lot, probably 100 outside vendors in total.

They feel that love too. They are also part of our family. The FedEx lady hugs me every time I see her. I cannot tell you how many vendors have told me that we're their favorite business to work with. And they're not really seeing me that much. It's not that they love me as a person, they see our staff, and our staff is an extension of me. The staff's attitude and positivity signal to everyone that this is a great place not only to do business, but to be a part of.

The ultimate reason that our vendors are a good source of recruitment is that everyone we hire aligns with our core values. All my employees treat our vendors with the same amount of respect as they would a customer, and they do this consistently because they exhibit our core values in all of their interactions.

The owner of Zappos was recently talking about customer service. He said, "I never train customer service, I only hire customer service." What this means is that the people he hires *are* customer service. They don't need to be trained to treat everyone with kindness and respect because that is who they are. I only hire individuals who have integrity, who love people, and who possess a servant attitude. Because they display these characteristics, they have created a fantastic relationship with our vendors, who then go out into the world and advertise on our behalf.

Early on, when I bought my first dealership, one of my friends went into business with me. He owned his own business and was smitten by mine. He came and worked with me for a little while and loved it, so we decided to partner and buy a store together as an extension of the one I already had. We installed someone to run his company, and he came and worked with me as we began seeking out another company to buy.

One day I was at the dealership, and a guy who had been in the car business for a long time came by to apply for a job. My friend waited on him in the parking lot, and the guy coming in essentially shrugged him off. He treated my friend as if he was not important because in his mind, I was the only one that mattered. He was coming to see me. He belittled my friend and didn't show him any interest. Little did he know that the opportunity he was applying for was working directly under my friend. It was kind of like an undercover boss situation, and it just so happened that my friend ended up being the one to serve him in the parking lot.

Well, the new guy gets to my office, and we sit down and start talking about the opportunity. He says, "I'd love to be a part of your company." Sugar could melt in his mouth, he was so sweet.

I said, "Well, I would love for you to meet my business partner because he's going to be the one running things." My friend walks into the room, and you could see the look on this guy's face. His jaw nearly dropped to the ground.

My friend is like, "Yeah. I met him outside." And you could see this guy nearly falling over himself. He didn't know what to say or what to do, and, of course, we did not end up hiring him.

At that time, we had not established our core values. We were still hiring based exclusively on talent. But he didn't meet our core values then, even though we didn't really know what our core values were. He was very talented, but he did not have a servant attitude.

How does this story tie together with using our vendors to recruit prospective employees? I hire people with the servant attitude. When you hire people who naturally treat others well, your relationships will grow. I know our vendors go out into the community and tell everyone how great our business is because they get the utmost respect from my employees every single time. They share those stories and attract more people with the servant attitude, and the pattern continues.

We're not the type of business that just fires people. We don't fire employees, and we don't fire vendors unless we have a good reason that we've communicated to them. People feel safe working for us because they know where they stand. They know if there was a problem, we would have already communicated it by now.

We had a store that was not doing great in cleanup. Immediately our managers were like, "This is crazy. This is a successful business; somebody should be doing a good job cleaning our facilities."

They got quotes for all of the different companies that work as vendors, and we tried to design a program that carves out a section of our business so that if something changes in the quality of service they're providing, we make sure they are notified. We didn't fire them right away; we created a method to hold them accountable so that they had an opportunity to fix their performance. I treat vendors the same as employees in all regards. If a vendor is not performing up to par, I make sure they understand what the path forward should look like. They need to understand what the deficiency is and what the consequences will be if the problem is not addressed.

We chart a course for success that includes how success is measured. It is only after all this is done, and still, nothing changes, that we will let anyone go or end our contract with any of our vendors.

One of the biggest vendors in any industry is advertising. In my industry, businesses spend millions of dollars a year on advertising. But in the beginning, I didn't really know what I was doing. You don't know what you don't know. I reached out to all of our vendors, every TV station and every radio station we dealt with, and asked all of them to get together with me in one room.

So WRL was with CBS, CBS was with ABC, ABC was with ESPN; we had representatives from all over in one of my little dealerships. I said, "Look, I love you all, but I am not smart enough to read between the lines on this stuff. I want you all to tell me, in this room today, what's the fairest way to compare you against each other? What's the fairest way?" As I got them to talk about it, they began to build a method of measuring themselves against one another.

And, of course, they started telling on each other, it was so great. They were like, "Well, the only way to really know is to look at what happened as opposed to what was sold." And here's the thing: Billions of dollars in advertising were sold to companies and individuals. Billions and billions of dollars. They never checked to see if the customer got what they paid for.

Now I know if I'm paying X amount of money for advertising, I want Y amount of people to see it, minimum. But that was never how it happened. Now with the internet it's different, but back when it was exclusively TV advertising, it was much harder to gauge. You would develop a relationship with the representative, and they would offer you free promotional things, meanwhile, you weren't actually getting anything that you paid for.

It's not that the advertiser wasn't trying to give you what they sold you. They weren't evil people. The problem was simply that no one ever checked. They were not looking at that data. Somebody else is putting it in the system, somebody else is creating the content, somebody else is plugging the timer. It's not that I think that the advertisers were trying to mislead me, but the communication was not clear, and there was no understanding when it came to what great looked like. I was just like a lost employee; I had no idea how to win. Eventually, I got all of my marketing vendors together so we could decide what great looked like. I was afraid that they would think I was an ass, but they ended up having respect for me. They respected that I could own the fact that I didn't know crap about advertising, but I was willing to understand and learn so I could hold them accountable.

So many businesses step on their vendors. They treat them as if they're not important, they're in the way, they're a disruption. I'm the exact opposite. So many people don't trust their vendors, they think they're out to get them. The vendors aren't out to get you, you just haven't established a trusting relationship. You haven't articulated exactly what it is you want, so they haven't been able to deliver. Establishing clear expectations is not only how you get what you want, but also how you build trust and show them they matter to your business.

> **Establishing clear expectations is not only how you get what you want, but also how you build trust and show them they matter to your business.**

I communicate and communicate honestly. If you're failing me as a vendor, I don't just fire you and get somebody else. I treat them the same way I would my employees. I would say, "Hey, look, this is what we agreed to, this is what's not happening, can you do it? Or do we need to go somewhere else?" That doesn't mean I'll wait forever, or I'll even have that conversation twice, but it will happen. Morally, that is at the center of everything I do in my company. Communication upfront, establishing clear expectations and measurements, and holding each other accountable to that agreement.

I would say that very few companies of our size think about their business partners that way. They think about what they bring to the bottom line, synergy, and all that. But we care about them, it's that simple. Our vendors know they matter to us, and because they know they matter to us, they'll bend over backward to serve our business. These FedEx reps and these industry-specific vendors go into all the other stores, and they talk to all the different people, and guess what happens? Someone will say, "Hey, I'm thinking about making a change. Where would you go?"

Well, that vendor is going to say, "There's no question where I'd go, I'd go to Hiester."

Vendors are a really significant recruiting tool. People feel the love when they walk through our doors, and they feel the love regardless of whether they're a customer of ours or we're customers of theirs. The feeling is the same.

CUSTOMERS BECOME EMPLOYEES

Any company worth their salt will tell you that they sell the vision of their company to customers. This makes sense, it is how you get the customer's business. What many people don't realize, however, is that customers can also be a valuable method of recruitment. It is the same principle as wanting my employees and vendors to go out into the world saying what a great place Hiester Automotive is to work.

Yes, I want customers to think, "Wow, they have excellent customer service. I am going to them for all my vehicle needs." But the ball doesn't stop there. I also want them to think, "All their staff members look so happy. It seems like a great place to work," which then becomes, "You know, so and so's daughter is looking for a job in sales, maybe she should try Hiester's." Of course, I want my customers to think of my business as a great place to do business, but I also want them to understand that it is a great place to work.

There have been numerous instances in which customers have not only connected us with people we eventually hired, but where we have hired the customer themselves.

> *I want my customers to think of my business as a great place to do business, but I also want them to understand that it is a great place to work.*

One of our employees is a valet driver at one of our stores. He was a customer of ours who retired and didn't need to go back to work. He literally came out of retirement to work for us, just because he wanted to be here every day. He said, "I just love this place and I want to be a part of it. So just give me a job."

People come to us just for the culture, just because it's a place that feels good. And that is where the heart of the matter lies: When you treat everyone as if they matter, everyone will want to be around you. They will come to work for you and send others to work for you, simply so they can be in a culture that makes them feel good, so that they can work with people they genuinely enjoy.

MARKET TO TARGET EMPLOYEES

The principle of everyone matters is so important that it has become the focal point of all of our advertising. Yes, we have competitive pricing, we offer great vehicles, and we have excellent work and training opportunities, but our real superpower as a company is our culture. The prices may bring customers in the same way that a job opportunity may bring in a prospective hire, but what keeps them coming back, customer and employee alike, is the culture.

One of the things that I've learned is that marketing is just as important when it comes to attracting prospective employees as it is to attracting customers. The way you market your business is going to give a first impression to people who might decide to come work for you, the same way it would customers. Whether this is TV advertising, internet advertising, or print media, it will impact prospective employees as much as prospective customers. The first impression I want prospective hires to have of my company is that we treat everyone with respect and enthusiasm. We let people know they matter to us.

Time and time again I hear parents, relatives, and friends say how great a company is based on

> *What keeps them coming back, customer and employee alike, is the culture.*

their advertising. Lately, Amazon has been using their marketing to show their investment in their employees' ability to go to college. They want to brand themselves as investing in their employees, and they do this in an effort to make you want to do business with them. In a way, they are reverse recruiting in their advertising.

What we have always done with our advertising is make sure it is consistent with our brand. This results in people who have never met me talking about how sincere we are. They don't know me, and they don't know my philosophy, but they can tell from our advertising and the way we do business that we prioritize our employees over money. It is so important to understand your brand because how you market your business not only speaks to your customer, but speaks to potential recruiters for your business and potential hires for your business.

It is important to keep your marketing simple and consistent. In our marketing, I choose to emphasize how our business has a great work environment where everyone treats each other well. This is what I want people to think of when they think of Hiester Automotive.

This is a helpful exercise for you to practice if you are trying to enhance your advertising, and I will discuss this more in the following chapter. Think about one or two qualities of your business that you think you have successfully implemented. These should be your high points, attractive parts of your business that you do exceptionally well. These should be the qualities you center your advertising around. Below is a list of examples of messaging you can sell in your advertising to keep your advertising as consistent as possible. Pick one or two characteristics to base your messaging on:

- Great pay
- Employee-centric business
- Inclusive benefits package
- Quality working conditions
- Flexible hours
- Remote work opportunities
- Amazing work culture
- Family-friendly
- Quality training
- Advanced education program
- Ideal location
- Unique job responsibilities

Whatever your strength is, you want to emphasize it and emphasize it consistently. When you market to prospective employees, it is not only about everything you can give them, but also about letting them know they matter to you. When potential hires know that you treat everyone as if they matter, they trust that they too will matter in your workplace.

CHAPTER 5

INTERVIEW EVERYONE

The interview is the pinnacle of the hiring process. It is the moment where you and the candidate get to sit down together and make your case to one another. I have illustrated in previous chapters the importance of selling the prospective hire on your vision for the company, and it is precisely for that reason that I choose to interview everyone. While not everyone who wants to work for our company gets hired, everyone gets an interview. If you have made it this far in the book, the reason why should not be surprising to you.

I love people. All of my managers love people. We want to get to know everyone to take the opportunity to share our vision for the company as widely as possible, even if that candidate is not the right fit for us. In my mind, interviews are one of the most potent, and certainly the most under-utilized, methods of recruitment.

In this chapter, I will not only be further explaining my philosophy for why I choose to interview everyone, but also some tactics I use in interviews to determine if a candidate fits the requirement for a position, as well as our core values. My hope is that you will come away with a different perspective on the interview process and what it can accomplish for your business.

AN OPPORTUNITY FOR RECRUITMENT

When a person is applying for a position at your business, there is always a reason. They were drawn in by your marketing, maybe they know someone that knows you, or perhaps they are in some way connected to your industry. They could have just randomly selected you because your position aligns with their experience, and they are looking for opportunities in your region. My way of approaching interviews is using them as an opportunity to share my vision of the company: who we are, our core values, our core focus, and why it is a great place to work.

Companies spend millions of dollars trying to advertise, trying to attract talent to their business. These days you can see "Now Hiring" or "Help

Wanted" on every gas station and restaurant. You see it on the TV; everywhere you look people are hiring. But people don't see interviews as an opportunity for recruitment, as an opportunity to share what your company is all about. Even if the person you are interviewing isn't the perfect candidate, even if you're not going to hire them, I never pass up on an opportunity to share who we are and what we do. I never pass up on an opportunity to send someone back out into the world thinking, "Man, I'd love to work there." Even if you hire in a completely different direction, it doesn't change the way that person feels about the time they got to spend with you or whoever is representing your company.

I believe discovering talent is one of the most important jobs I have as the leader of my organization. Historically, most leaders think of it as 1% of the job, but in reality, it's closer to 40%. What a lot of leaders don't realize is not only how important hiring is, but how much easier their job would be if they did it right.

My philosophy for hiring is this: Life is a series of connections. It's like a spider web. Every person you meet has the potential to be connected to your business, whether it be through a relative, a customer you already serve, or an employee that works within your organization. Everything is a series of connections, and when you think about recruitment that way, everyone you meet becomes a potential asset to your company.

When you walk through life attuned to these connections, you won't believe how many doors open. I can't tell you how many people I run into who have sent their kids to work for me. It happens just like this: I'll run into a friend and ask, "How's your kid doing?"

"Well, he's confused. He's not sure what he wants to do." Or, "She thought she wanted to go in this direction, but now she's in between things."

And I'll say, "Well, look, I've got some really neat programs for recent college graduates. Send her over to look at them. If nothing else, she can see what we are all about."

A few years back, I went to Marshalls to buy some arcade game consoles that were at a reduced price after the holidays. I got to talking with the girl who was helping me. She had just graduated from college and didn't know what she wanted to do. Four years later, she works for me, and we just promoted her to a managerial position.

Most managers and leaders make their decision on whether they hire a candidate in the first five minutes. The moment you walk in the door and start talking, the manager is making a decision. Traditional companies make that decision quickly, and they spend the rest of the time either trying to convince you to work there or trying to get rid of you. They'll say, "Oh, I've got a call," or, "Oh, I'm sorry I have this thing," or they will straight up tell you, "You're not right for this position." There is nothing wrong with this approach. It gets the job done.

But I have a completely different philosophy. My belief is that there is no better time to recruit and develop your body of applicants than in an interview. The amount of people who want to come work for you is dependent on the amount of people you talk to about coming to work for your company. This is why I interview everyone, because every interview is an opportunity to network and build connections.

> **Every interview is an opportunity to network and build connections.**

This is especially important for small businesses. My company started out very small. We didn't have a formal brand, we just had a reputation in our community. We didn't have the large quantities of people wanting to work for our organization the way we do today. In the beginning, we had no choice but to interview everyone. And what that small-scale operation teaches you is that while this candidate may not be the person you want, they have those valuable connections in the community nonetheless. A lot of the people we ended up with came from folks we met in those initial interviews.

Applying this practice gives oneself the ability to access fish in a bigger pond, like we discussed earlier. Most people settle for what they get because they don't know how to develop anything better. But we take the time upfront to understand what great looks like in this position and create a demand in the market by advertising to every single person we talk to. If somebody comes in to interview for a job, whether they are the right person or the wrong person, my job as the manager is to sell them on the vision of our company so that they leave that room wanting to be a part of it.

Thinking back to earlier chapters, I talked about how important it is to use the right employee to conduct your interviews. They have to be able to share the vision of the company with the same passion you would as the founder or CEO. They have got to see the vision so clearly that when they are in the interview room, the prospective hire can practically taste it. They have to be able to see exactly what you are trying to accomplish, the direction you are going, and how you are going to get there. They need to see the passion of the person doing the interview. They need to know the person hiring is passionate about what they do and where they work.

Hiring people is the same principle as serving customers. Bad salespeople pre-qualify customers. They make a determination early in the conversation and decide that this person is not a good customer. This practice is called pre-qualifying, and I have seen it my entire life. There are certain qualifiers someone needs to possess in order to be an ideal customer. An example in the car industry would be not having good credit. Whatever it is, salespeople will make a determination, not based on fact but on opinion or outward visual signs, and end up missing someone who could be a valued customer.

I don't ever want to pre-qualify someone. I want to take the time to get to know them and see if there is a place within our company where they can fit. And if there isn't, can I help them find a place that works for them? You would be amazed at how many people I have helped find work somewhere else, and they keep in touch and say, "If you ever have an opportunity, please keep me in mind." Lo and behold, a perfect opportunity emerges, and they come to work for me. I see situations like that every day. It comes down to one simple question: Do you care enough to get to know someone even if they are not right for a position? And sadly, most people don't.

This is why it's mind-boggling to me that companies will spend millions on advertising when they have a captive audience that comes into their business every day for an interview, yet they are not going to take the time to talk and share their vision. Why not seize that opportunity? The interview is free advertising. Take advantage of it, spread your vision, and build your reputation in your community. Do this, and you won't have to settle on an employee. Instead, you'll have a line of them out the door.

CREATE YOUR OWN RUMOR

If 10 people want to come work for you, you get to choose from 10 people. If two people want to work for you, you have to choose from two. The idea is to make everyone want to work for you, and then you have the opportunity to truly find the best candidate from a wide range of options. They may not be perfect for my company, but they could be working next to the guy that is, so either way I want you to leave talking about how highly you think of my business.

I'll give an example of why this philosophy is so important. Let's say there is a mechanic working in a shop across town. They interviewed for a position at my company, but I decided not to hire them. They still sit with the other mechanics at that company. They still see their colleagues every day. Five of those employees might be people I really want to hire. It would be great if one of their own could come back saying, "Man, if I could go anywhere, it would be Hiester Automotive."

> **The more you work to spread a positive message about your company, the more incoming talent you are likely to have.**

I use mechanics as an example because it is specific to my industry, but the principle is the same no matter what you do. If you're a roofer, a painter, an accountant, a banker, no matter what it is, the more people who go out into the world saying, "If I could work anywhere, it would be there," the easier it is going to be to attract talent. It all connects back to the same theory: The more you work to spread a positive message about your company, the more incoming talent you are likely to have.

What you're doing here is starting your own rumor. You are creating a positive rumor about your company. As I stated in the previous section, I form meaningful connections with everyone I meet and use it as an opportunity to share my vision of my company. But what does that actually mean? What am I promoting when I talk about my company?

There is a strategy to this. Take a few facts that you can communicate consistently across your brand and pick your high points. Attorneys do this in the court of law all the time. They take key points from their argument, and they drive them home so strongly that people can't see anything but those points. Branding is essentially the same practice. Pick your high points and share them with everyone you interview; share them with your managers and tell them to pass them on. The simpler and more straightforward the messaging is, the more consistent it will be when relayed.

In advertising they say, "Repetition, repetition, repetition." It takes multiple times for a message to resonate, otherwise, it is just a banner flashing by. I give my companies high points to everyone, especially prospective employees. That way people begin to hear your name along with quality jobs, and they associate the two. Soon it becomes a fact that everyone knows and acknowledges: "Hiester Automotive has great job opportunities."

Another facet of my company I love to share with people is our philanthropic presence in the community. I wanted to create a facet of our organization that put our core values into practice and was committed to giving back to the community. Because of that mission, we created the Hiester Cares Foundation. The Hiester Cares Foundation works to serve underprivileged youth in our community, as well as those suffering from drug addiction.

We are constantly trying to hone our focus and level up the impact we can have on underserved and less fortunate individuals. It has become clear that having a practice such as this is becoming increasingly important to prospective hires. Simply put, candidates want to know they are going to work for an organization that has skin in the game.

My question to you is this: What are you doing to give back that you can share with a prospective employee to truly show them where the rubber meets the road for your organization? In other words, if I am applying for jobs and trying to make a decision between two organizations, does being with a company that has a large philanthropic presence impact my decision? For me, it most certainly does. I urge you as a business owner to ask what your company is doing to give back. That may help make the decision for someone on the fence about whether they should come to work for you.

It is important to note that I am not suggesting you

use your philanthropic endeavors for monetary gain. For example, we never advertise how much money we give to charity or what causes we have allied ourselves with. Rather, we share this vision with prospective hires because we genuinely want employees who share these values and can be a part of this practice and can further our impact in the community.

Whether it is philanthropy, opportunities for career growth, or expansive health care and benefits, select your company's strongest points and make sure everyone around you knows that your company is committed to providing these for your potential hires. That is how you create a rumor in your community that will inevitably attract quality talent to your door.

THE STAPLER

When I first got into the automobile business, I interviewed at a company where the manager considering me ended up being my boss later in life. Not in this situation, because I didn't get the job, as you'll soon see why, but later on.

I walked into the interview, and I was talking to the guy, and he asked me to sell him a stapler. He said, "Alright, John. I own a company. We employ 230 office personnel, and I'm constantly having to replace staplers, and I'm getting frustrated about it. I have reached out to your company and asked them to send me a salesperson, here you are. Tell me about your staplers." He had me role play with it. He said, "Walk into the room as if you're a salesman coming to sell staplers. Take as long as you need to review the stapler."

He had some specific things he was looking for in that sales process. He wanted to see me make eye contact, the way I shook hands, did I have a dominant or subservient handshake? He had thought about things of that nature and identified what he wanted in advance. Now, the reason I didn't get this job should be clear to any person with sales experience; I immediately went to the product. I told him about the copper outside and the staples, and this and that. But I didn't ask him a single question. I didn't ask him what his needs were, what about the stapler was frustrating him, what was breaking, etc. I went to sell him a product without fully understanding what his needs were. In all sales situations, it's about building a case for your product. You need to ask questions that lead you to a place where you can serve them. I failed miserably at that interview, but I learned a lot.

> *In all sales situations, it's about building a case for your product. You need to ask questions that lead you to a place where you can serve them.*

For years, I have used that same exercise when interviewing salespeople, and you can too. Every position is different, and my style of interview is a bit unconventional. The reason for this is because the initial interview is really me selling the vision of our company to the prospective employee. I want to choose from as many candidates as possible, so the initial interview is always me trying to make them want to come back. Well, if you interviewed 10 people and only one of them wants to come to work for you, you have to decide if you want to settle for that one person or not. If you interview 10 people and all 10 of them want to come to work for you, now you get to make an intelligent and informed decision about which person fits the predetermined attributes for that seat.

I always teach that your first mission in an interview, in addition to getting to know the person, is to make sure that you've sold them on what your vision is so that they want to come to work at your company. I think there are two parts to any good interview: me selling to you and you selling to me. I always make sure my people have sold the vision of the company, who we are, and why this person should want to come work here.

This is part of why I choose to interview everyone, because even if they aren't the right fit right now, they are still one more person to whom I get the opportunity to sell our vision. And who knows, maybe their uncle is a future customer, or their best friend comes in for an interview next time we have an opening. For me, interviews are an excellent way to get to know people and for them to get to know me. And I love my company, so why wouldn't I want to share the vision with everybody, even those we don't end up hiring?

Interviewing everyone has so many tangible benefits to your company. It allows you to share your vision, it gives you a broader pool of potential candidates, and it weeds out those who don't fit your core values. Many may think of interviewing people who aren't the right fit as a waste of time. But if you share with them the enthusiasm and love you have for your company, I promise it will make hiring down the line infinitely easier, because you will never be short on people who want to work for you.

SCENARIOS

Interviewing everyone means, unfortunately, that sometimes you are going to have people come in who simply don't fit. This could be for a whole host of reasons: they could not have the right experience, maybe their strengths don't align with what the position requires, or they could simply have a bad attitude. I like to use scenarios to ensure the candidate aligns with what great looks like in that position.

Scenarios allow you to see how the prospective hire operates under pressure. If you have any hesitations about the candidate, it can help you gauge whether those hesitations have merit. When you don't take the time to speak with someone and judge based on assumptions, you open yourself up to the risk of losing someone who could add real value to your business. At best, interviewing everyone finds you an excellent employee; at worst, you can make an informed decision as to why someone doesn't fit.

At best, interviewing everyone finds you an excellent employee; at worst, you can make an informed decision as to why someone doesn't fit.

In the interview room, I like to put them in situations where either conflict or opportunity arises, and they have to figure out what they would do in that situation. I'm at a point in my career where the only people I'm hiring personally are managers. I'll take tough employee situations or opportunities and say, "You're in this situation. Here's what you've got up to this point. What would you do if you were me? What would you say if you were me?"

I've always felt like it's not only good from an interview process, but also from a management process too. Because what it forces you to do is try to think like somebody else in order to solve a problem. So down the road, if you have somebody who's making a request and you're looking at it thinking, "Well, I'm not sure how we got here," you are in the habit of thinking about the situation from the other person's perspective, and you can realize how the situation came to pass. A lot of times managers will solve their own problems this way. They'll move from disagreement to, "I get what you're saying."

If I have a manager who is struggling with an employee not listening to them, not respecting their authority, sure, they can yell at them or berate them, but that never leads to a more positive working relationship. I train my managers to think about it from the employee's perspective before they even get the job. So that rather than escalate an already tense situation, they know how to think, "If I were them, and I wasn't listening, what would I need to hear in order for me to get in line? What would my manager need to say for me to respect and listen to them?"

Scenarios are effective because they give the potential employee an opportunity to address any concerns or hesitancies you may have in hiring them. The more you know about the position, the prospective employee, and how the two align, the better-catered scenarios you can ask them. Scenarios should be catered to the position, not only to determine who would be the best fit, but also to prepare that candidate for real-world conflicts they may have to navigate.

A good example of this is an interview I went into with a guy who has gone on to become one of our Parts Managers. He was quite a bit younger than anyone else we had employed in that position, and it is a big job. The Parts Managers run a large operation, and he had previously worked for a much smaller business. Because I knew these things going into the interview and had specific areas I wanted him to address, I created scenarios that reflected them.

I told him, "Look, you're likely going to be in a situation where your colleagues have been in the business a long time and will have more experience than you. How do you feel about developing and training them?"

I remember it like it was yesterday. He said, "I have a vision for what the department could look like. My expectation is that the people in those positions have two or three screens and are sourcing from multiple operations. They need to be able to process data quickly."

His response told me that he wasn't just telling me what I wanted to hear. He was describing a vision of what he thought this department should be like. To this day, he is still with my company, and he has arguably made the largest impact on his department of anyone we have had in the last two or three years. The reason for this is that he has held true to his vision.

Looking back, I had understandable reasons to be concerned about how he would handle the responsibilities of this position. But he was capable of taking the time to develop his relationship with each of his employees and to get their buy-in for his vision. He helped them to understand why this was so important and what we were trying to accomplish. Most of the employees who worked under him are still with us or have actually moved on to other jobs that incorporate the skills they learned from him.

I left that meeting completely impressed. This candidate was not only someone who fit our core values, but believed so strongly in his vision that he wasn't afraid to share it with me. After that, I had no doubts about hiring because I knew if he could sell me on his vision, he could sell it to his employees.

I also use the scenarios to see if they fit who we are and align with our core values.

One situation I often use is this: You have an employee who is a top producer, they make you all the money in the world, and they have mistreated another employee. It's not an instance of abuse or anything like that, but they've been short with them and made them feel like an outcast. What do you do in that situation? You can get a sense right away of how that person is going to handle conflict. Do they ask more questions?

People will ask, "Is the employee a top producer too? Or are they a newbie?" If they start asking things like that, I know right away they don't fit us because they are thinking that being a top performer exempts someone from right and wrong. I try to use situations like that to tell me what I need to know without coming out and asking directly.

Another thing I will always ask is what they liked

and disliked about their previous job. If someone can tell me what they admired about a place they no longer work, that is a good framework for me. That tells me that they love people; even if things didn't end the way they wanted, they are still able to see the positives. But if someone says, "There was nothing I liked...I worked next to somebody I couldn't stand," you know that individual doesn't love people. And you realize pretty quickly that perhaps they have had problems in more than one place.

If they said something a little more vague, maybe something like, "My boss and I didn't see eye-to-eye," that is a good opportunity to ask prompting questions such as, "What would you have done differently in that situation?" or, "What would you have done if the roles were reversed?" You can learn a lot about people when you ask them about previous work experiences. I don't want an employee who is always going to blame problems on other people. I am looking for someone who can try to see the situation from another perspective or who can take a certain amount of responsibility.

PROCESS OUT THE FLAKES

It's funny. Recently, Ashley, who owns the bakery, was speaking at a Rotary event in town. The Rotary Club buys breakfast from her for their events, and so they asked if she would come share her story for them. Watching her speak, she made me look bad. She was so good. There was actually a man in the Rotary Club who owned a bakery right around the corner from hers. The event was a panel, so after sharing her story she began answering questions. Well, this guy asked her, "What do you do when you've hired a flake?"

She asked, "What do you mean?"

And he said, "You know, you've hired someone, and they don't come in on time, they don't do this or that."

And she said, "Well, we don't hire flakes. We have established our core values upfront; we know what works well for us. We may interview them because we interview everyone, but if someone wants to work for us, they need to embody our core values or else they won't get in the door."

He's sitting there speechless, and I was like, "Wow. She's better than I am."

I was so proud. I'm glad she picked up on the philosophy of interviewing everyone because I really believe in it. I believe our lives are all connected, and just because it may not be the right time or right position for this person doesn't mean they don't play an important role in your business later on.

Now, with that being said, I certainly wouldn't want to waste anybody's time. From the job listing, I'm going to clearly communicate what we are looking for, and if they don't fit, most people will make the decision on their own not to come in. But if someone reaches out and says they are looking for a job, even if I don't need anyone specific, I'm going to interview them. I'll say, "Well, hey, let's get together for a cup of coffee." And we'll talk because I am never going to miss an opportunity to spread the vision of my company, especially when a person reaches out and expresses an interest. I am going to take the opportunity to tell them what we are all about. I can't tell you how many people I have spoken to at one point or another where even if they don't end up coming to work for us then, years down the line they'll find themselves looking for a job and remember, "Hiester has a great company. Hiester has a great work environment. Let me reach out to him and see if he's hiring."

A few months ago, Ashley had a girl resign who had been with her since the beginning, so she was trying to fill the position. And because she is my daughter, and she has seen how I run my business, she went through all the steps. She took the time to write down what great looks like for that position, and she had her company's core values set. One night she was trying to decide between three people.

She asked me for my advice, and I looked at her and said, "Have you graded each of them based on your criteria?" We looked at the criteria she had put in the job listing, and she gave each person a score out of 10 for each of those criteria. Then I said, "Have you graded each of them based on your core values?" She did it again but this time with her core values. By the time we finished, it was very easy to decide who to hire. There was one person who stood above the others in terms of aligning with her criteria and core values. When you don't know what you want it can be hard to make a judgment like that. But when you are explicit about what great looks like, it becomes a lot clearer.

In no way does "Interview Everyone" mean "Hire Everyone." We are very selective about who we hire, and we don't hire anyone who is not in line with our core values. I have created stopgaps within my company so that there is a system of checks and balances when it comes to hiring. We have a General Manager who does the second interview; it is their responsibility to ensure that every hire is appropriate for the position they are being put in. I am in no way saying we never make mistakes. There are always going to be instances where someone may deceive you, but the more stopgaps that are put in place, the less likely that is to happen.

Small businesses often prioritize filling positions over the quality of the people they hire. When filling a position is the end goal, you allow yourself to potentially hire people who aren't a good fit for your company – they're flakes. Then you settle, and more often than not, that is the biggest mistake a business can make. We have these

> **Small businesses often prioritize filling positions over the quality of the people they hire.**

stopgap measures in place to ensure that we never settle. The General Manager has to sign off on every single hire so that there is a fresh pair of eyes. And the GM knows that they won't have to work extra hours if this person is not hired; they won't have to stay late or do twice the work. The GM is not going to be impacted by whether or not the position is filled, so they have no motivation to settle for less or hire out of desperation.

Everyone who interviews for our company undergoes a core value assessment. This is a piece of their interview process. We ask questions that prompt answers on our core values: Character/Integrity, Love People, Possess a Get-It-Done Attitude, Professionalism, and Possess a Servant Attitude. It also falls on whoever is hiring to make it clear why it is so important that all of our employees embody these characteristics. A good example of an interview question we ask is this: "Of these core values, which one best and least describes you?" I like this question because it reveals a lot about the individual. It is the kind of question that simply doesn't allow the candidate to only tell you what they think you want to hear.

We've got over 300 employees; I can't hire everyone myself anymore. One thing I do is create videos for my staff who conduct interviews. I teach through these videos, so that no matter who is conducting the interview, they do it as I would. I like to illustrate the interview process on video and note the important things that need to happen. I emphasize the core-value assessment, sharing the company's long-term vision, etc. I make sure my employees know the things that need to happen in every interview. If someone slips through the cracks, and we end up hiring someone who doesn't fit, I can point to the exact part of the interview process that the employee didn't do or didn't monitor carefully enough.

Training videos are a very helpful tool that we have adopted as a company. We use an HRIS system called Paycor that allows us to create digital learning. If there is a topic we need anyone in our company to be trained on, instead of trying to coordinate a Zoom training, we shoot a video and get it to the masses immediately. I'll get on the video and say, "Hey guys, look, we met today to talk about these things, and this is a summary of what we decided as a group. There are some questions about how we handle X, Y, and Z, and I want to assure you that we've put a lot of thought into this, and this is the direction we would like to go. If you have any input, please... I'm here, you can contact me anytime." We then put the videos in their learning portal, and it becomes a required watch form for that position. We can also see if it's actually been viewed the entire way through and not just the first two minutes. This is a great way to create consistent practices within the company.

Now, you may be reading this and thinking, "Well, if I follow all of these practices, I'm never going to be able to hire anybody!" And if you have only one or two applicants, you're right. But if you have interviewed everyone, sold all of them on the vision, and have 10 people to choose from, these practices are going to allow the clear candidate to rise to the top. All of these practices tie together into a larger framework through putting methods in place to make sure we have as many candidates to choose from as possible, and we are able to find the best possible fit for that position.

CHAPTER 6

CHOOSE FIT OVER TALENT

Core values, when implemented correctly, have the possibility to completely change your company. When I say implemented correctly, I don't mean hung on the wall and then ignored or referenced only when it is convenient. I mean having every decision related to your business be in service of these values. When done correctly, your core values can create a unity and stability in your company that allow you to constantly have diligent and dedicated employees who stay on for long periods of time, if not for the rest of their careers.

These values are Character/Integrity, Loves People, Possess a Get-it-Done Attitude, Professionalism, and Possess a Servant Attitude. They started off as simply what I wanted to see in ideal candidates.

In my first book, *Why Jacob Matters*, I describe in great detail how we went about developing and defining our core values. In the beginning, they were simply what we used to evaluate who we hire and who we don't. But over time, it has become a promise I make to employees that I will surround them with people who embody these characteristics.

But there is another side of that as well. My employees understand, like I understand, that in order to fulfill that promise, we need to constantly exhibit these traits. If we want and expect our colleagues to behave this way, we have to behave that way as well. What this creates is a uniform ideal everyone strives towards and a work environment that truly makes people happy.

My son-in-law who worked in banking eventually came to work for me. He's been here about two years and is doing an amazing job. The other employees are all really engaged with him, they have accepted him, and they don't even think about him being related to me because he holds his own as an employee. We were having a conversation recently, and I asked him, "If we weren't in this business, and we could do anything, what business would you choose? What would you want to do?"

He said, "Let me think about it."

A few days later, he got back to me.

He said, "I can honestly say that I can't possibly imagine a place or a business I'd rather work in than the one we're in right now." He said, "The people want to be here. They want to make it great, they want to jump in. When a problem happens, the first thing they do is jump in and say, 'Hey, how can I help?' I absolutely love what I'm doing."

Hiring talented people will make your company money, but hiring employees who fit with your mission and core values will create a unified environment where everyone wants to help the business succeed.

CHARACTER AND INTEGRITY

Our business used to hire people based on their talent. If you were a great mechanic, you could work here. If you were a great salesman, you could work here. The problem with that approach is that it doesn't take the group dynamic into account. There was no consideration for whether or not an employee fit our company. What became abundantly clear was that having a great mechanic who didn't fit with the rest of our people was just having a bad mechanic.

> *Having a great salesman who didn't fit with the rest of our people was a bad salesman.*

Having a great salesman who didn't fit with the rest of our people was a bad salesman. We stopped hiring based on talent first and started making our core values the priority.

Character and integrity are part of our core values. When I am looking at a prospective employee, they have to have character. I want empowered people. I want people who think for themselves, who are self-motivated. Every manager wants that. But what a lot of managers also want is to put people under their thumb, and believe me, that is the last thing you want to do. What I want from my prospective employees is the kind of people I can equip to win. I want people who, no matter what the situation is, are going to get the job done. I want someone who is always striving to improve at their job, they don't just hole up with no concern for growth. I want an employee who will do the right thing, even when it doesn't provide them with personal gain.

We talk a lot as a team about how to identify character and integrity, and I give this example to illustrate exactly what I'm looking for. Let's say you're a sales manager with my organization. You go out to your car, and the spoiler is hanging down. It needs a clip to hold it on. You walk down to our parts department, and you say, "Hey, I need this clip, my spoiler's falling down."

The parts person says, "Here you go."

You say, "How much do I owe you?"

They say, "No, no, no, just take it."

You get to make a decision right then, and your decision is, "Am I going to take this opportunity to establish that I am a person of character, or am I going to take advantage of my situation?"

And my point is that you've only got so many opportunities in life to sell the rest of the world on your character.

This is a moment where you can stop and say, "Hey, look, I greatly appreciate it, but John's done a lot for me, I certainly don't want to take advantage of him. Please let me pay you for it. How much do I owe you?"

What happens when you walk away from that person in that scenario is they think, "Wow, that's a stand-up person."

Well, under normal circumstances, if you would had taken the free thing, it probably wouldn't have changed their opinion about you, but when it came time to decide who's the person within our company that's the best suited for the next level, and we're asking your peers, that person may step up and say, "Well, I'm going to tell you something, he's going to do the right thing, here's a scenario," and they're going tell that story.

I think back in my career where there were some opportunities for me to establish character and integrity. I used to host a sealed-bid auction at the dealership I now own. Wholesale dealers from around the city would bring stuff in. They would come look at the cars and turn in a sealed bid. Well, I had a guy come to see me one time who said, "Hey, look, I really need this one vehicle for a customer of mine, how about you just make my bid the top bid? I don't want to get it any cheaper than anybody else, if you just make mine the top bid, I'll get you a new big screen TV."

This is a true story. I worked for somebody else at the time. It wasn't my business; I was a sales manager. The way I saw it, it wasn't even my decision to make. If you own your own business, you can choose to run it as you see fit. But that wasn't within my rights as an employee. I looked at him, and I said, "What?"

He said, "No, I don't mean... Nothing bad. I'll just have the TV delivered to your house."

And I said, "You know what, get out." I looked at him, and I said, "Leave now."

And he was like, "Wait a minute, I'm not saying anything, I'm not trying to get it cheaper than anybody else. I'm willing to pay more, I just need it."

I said, "Look, get out, leave right now." I walked around the counter and said, "Go."

And about that time, the guy that had ridden with him came up and he said, "Hey, what's going on?"

I said, "Listen, if you're with him, you can leave too."

He said, "Woah, woah, woah, I just rode with him, I'm not with him. We're two different businesses."

I said, "Well, he's trying to bribe me so that he can get a vehicle, and I don't do business that way. It stands on its own. I'd appreciate it, if you're his ride, that you get him out of here right now."

To make a long story short, six years later I bought a dealership and was moving it into the town that both of those two ran businesses in. I built the new building, and we were opening that business.

I went to a chamber event, because that's the first thing we do to get to know the community, and there's a buzz, and they said, "Well, we don't really know you per se, but we know about you."

I said, "Oh, really? What's that?"

They said, "Well, we know that we can trust you, that you're a man of character."

And I was thinking, "How could you know that? How could you possibly know that? I'm just a normal person."

They said, "Well, we heard the auction story."

I said, "What?"

Everybody in town knew it before I ever even opened my business there, so you can see where that one incident six years earlier carried so much weight because I had the opportunity to do the right thing and took it. I can't tell you how much money it made me in the long term. Those are two examples of character and integrity. Make no mistake, when I made that decision, I had no idea it would impact my future in the way that it did. I was just trying to do the right thing.

THE SERVANT ATTITUDE

Another important concept for us is the servant attitude. We believe that you have to be a person that puts other people before yourself to work here and succeed. It doesn't mean that you can't succeed if you're focused on yourself, but to fit us as a company, we believe that you have to be the type of person that puts other people before yourself. It is this behavior that makes someone an asset to this company, that makes them an active player in moving our mission forward.

> **We believe that you have to be the type of person that puts other people before yourself.**

Professionally, we believe that everybody that works in our company needs to have the desire to be more than they are. A question I often get asked is, "How do you get buy-in from employees?" Or, "How do you get them involved?" Well, it's simple. We promise the people that come to work with our company that we're going to surround them with people that embody these core values and these characteristics.

There have been many situations where we have employees that we call high performers. And I love coaching and managing extremely talented individuals, but for most people, it's really hard. The reason it's hard is that this person is outperforming everybody on your team, so they become arrogant. They think they can mistreat other people, or they want special treatment.

We have had several instances where the top salesman at another organization wanted to come work for us. I remember one situation where my managers interviewed an individual from a different company and found he did not fit our core values, so, of course, we didn't hire him. For weeks afterward, he was calling me saying, "John, listen. I sell 30, 40 cars a month. I could make your business a lot of money. I can't believe your people won't hire me."

I had to tell him, "Look, I appreciate what you're saying, but in our organization, money is not the primary motivation for hiring. It's about whether you fit the other people on our staff. It sounds like, in this instance, it is not a good fit."

What I teach my managers and hold them accountable to is that there is right and there is wrong, and wrong takes you down a path of working somewhere else. When I first began implementing our core values, it was a way to identify talented people. But over the years, it has become so much more than that. It has become a promise to my employees that I'm going to surround them with people who embody those characteristics. If I make that promise and all of sudden I have a super performer that I'm not holding to that standard, I'm not loving them or the other people. If I tolerate someone who is not embodying the servant attitude, I am not serving my other employees the way I said that I would.

LOVE PEOPLE

I should care just as much about the high performer's growth as I do about the poor performer. It's easy to hold a poor performer accountable because their material improvement means the material success of your company, and it's easy to see where opportunity for growth is. But when it comes to a high performer, it becomes tempting to let them get away with whatever they want, and it can seem, at least temporarily, like that is what's in both of your self-interests.

But the truth is, it's not in their best interest, because no matter how well they perform now, they are clearly exhibiting a negative behavior that will ultimately limit their growth. If you go back to where I talk about loving people, this is exactly what I mean. I want them to be so important. I want their success and growth to be so important that I'm willing to lose them rather than let them do something that's not in their best interest. Because in the long term, what is in the best interest of our employees is always in the best interest of the company.

Our definition of "loving people" is not candy and roses, it is accountability. It's the mentality of, "I'm going to love everybody that works here as if they're my kid, as if their future matters so much to me that to let them continue to play in the street, knowing there's a chance they're going to get run over by a car, is asinine." If I've got to

> **Our definition of "loving people" is not candy and roses, it is accountability.**

punish them to get them to realize that they can't continue in that behavior, then that is what I have to do. But there are other ways that you can hold them accountable. Maybe it's you sending them home to think about it. Maybe it's something else.

So many people are afraid to do that because they think, "Well, they're going to go home and go look for a new job." So what? If it's in their best interest for them to do that, then they need to do that.

But if they want to be a part of this—and I hope that we've done a good enough job to make them want to be a part of it—then they're going to go home and recognize the promise that I made them, that I'd surround them with people that embody those characteristics. They're not going to find that somewhere else. I get it, I get it all the time from my employees, but it's what I believe is right. I believe so much in what we have that you'd be crazy not to want to be a part of it.

I believe that truly loving someone means holding them accountable. Love and accountability are not mutually exclusive. In fact, they don't even simply coexist; love and accountability reinforce one another. It is because I love my employees that the right decision is made so much clearer. When you put the love of your employee first, you can trust your actions are coming from the right place, and you don't have to worry about losing them. Sure, some people might respond negatively to being held accountable, but then they are no longer the right fit for us. The employees that fit will recognize we are holding them accountable because we love them and put in the work to change their behavior.

LEARN TO FAIL FAST

I have talked a lot about how to identify the right people, but identifying the wrong people is just as important. I believe that if someone was the right fit when we hired them, they will usually be the right fit down the line. But that doesn't always happen. If you hire someone and it quickly becomes clear they are not the right match for our company, learn to fail quickly. You have to care enough to have a conversation with them so that they know it is easier to find a job while they have a job. If they can't change their behavior, this is not the place for them.

> **If you hire someone and it quickly becomes clear they are not the right match for our company, learn to fail quickly.**

In business, you have to learn to fail fast. If the signs are there that the interview process did not weed out the wrong people, or if someone slips through the cracks, you need to stop kidding yourself. I don't care if they are an excellent performer; if they don't adhere to our core values, they need to leave.

It's like buying an item of clothing. If you buy something that is supposed to be a 36-inch waist, and when it arrives you see it's 32 inches, you're not going to keep it. You can't hold on to it and try to wear it. You're going to send it back. That's the same thing you have to do in the hiring process. If a person has been with you for a while and they've just gone off the rails somehow, then it's your obligation to stop and communicate that in a way that they understand. You need to take the time to make sure they know exactly what's expected of them and that they've been given every opportunity to succeed within your organization.

I never fire anybody that doesn't know they're going to be fired, unless there is an extreme case of insubordination. If I've hired the right person and they've made it through a certain period of time, but then begin to fall in their performance, I sit down with them personally and say, "Hey, look, this is what you agreed to, this is what we've asked of you, this is what's not happening."

I'll ask, "Are you in the wrong position? Do we need to look elsewhere in the organization for a different position?" If that is not the case, I'll ask, "Do you need to find a job while you're still employed? Because if we can't do it the way we've agreed to, this isn't going to work." For most people, that exposes their behavior. It forces them to be honest about whether they are not right for this specific position, or if they are not right for our company as a whole.

For me, a bad conversation with one of my direct reports is when they have had to let somebody go, or somebody's come to them and quit, and it's a surprise. A lot of people will just accept this; it's my job as a leader to make sure everyone is a right fit. An unexpected fire or unexpected quit is an indication that I am failing at ensuring my employees are the right kind of people, and if they are the right kind of people, they are getting what they need in order to stay.

I understand that there are always jobs that need doing, and you have to have a certain talent level or staffing level to satisfy your customer. But in my eyes, I'd rather stay small and get the right person in that seat than allow somebody to work in a position where they're failing. I don't want to continue to waste their time and not capitalize on their talent. I want all my employees to reach the level they want to reach. If that means moving someone around so that they can succeed, I'll do it. If that means firing someone who is not aligned with the rest of our company and our values, I'll do it.

Very few people take a job trying to screw up. I really believe that. Most people take a job wanting to impress, wanting to make a difference, wanting to contribute, and I don't care who it is. There may be a .1% exception to this, but 99.9% of the time, people want to please and they want to impress. Now, if they're not doing that, I'd say 80% of the time it's because you haven't communicated to them what is needed for them to succeed in that position.

It's unconventional, but in my view, making sure all my employees fit with my core values and mission ensures the long-term success of my company. And that's the way to maintain the employees I already have—by not letting the wrong people work among them. That's the way I do it every time, and that's the way I require my managers to do it every time. I'm here to build people. My whole job is to develop and grow individuals; that's my joy in life. I've made enough money. Money is great, it's a trophy for my success, but at the end of the day, my job is to make sure that everybody becomes all they can be. Throwing someone into a lake and saying, "Figure out how to swim," is never going to work. Neither is sticking someone in a position and saying, "Do your job."

Sometimes an employee who doesn't fit slips through the cracks. It is inevitable no matter how finely tuned your system is. The best thing you can do in that situation is fail fast, fire them quickly, and learn from the mistake. But just as important is being able to differentiate between an employee who doesn't fit from one who has simply fallen off in their performance. If they were right when you hired them, they likely are still right, and something else has gone wrong. In that case, you as a manager need to identify the problem, take accountability, and be agile enough to find a solution that will allow your employee to perform at their best.

LIVE THE CULTURE YOU WANT

Early on when we established our core values, it became apparent to us that it wouldn't only impact our hiring process, but that we had to measure the employees we had against those core values. I realized that my highest-performing service writer didn't fit; they were behaving in a way that didn't align with our core values. This is always tough, but as an owner, operator, or in any position of leadership, you have to be real about the situation. If you're going to conform to the culture that you want, you have got to make some of these tough decisions.

I met with this employee, and I got his evaluation, and we sat down. I said, "Hey, look. These are our core values: Character/Integrity, Love People, Possess a Get-it-Done Attitude, Professionalism, and Possess a Servant Attitude. You do really well in this core value and this core value, but you're failing in these two and if you can't change that, you can't work here. What I want you to recognize is if you can't figure out how to perform within a way that aligns with these core values, it's going to be easier for you to find a job while you have a job. If you know you can't change, you should go get that job now."

We gave him a reasonable amount of time to comply, and he didn't. We parted ways. I bear no ill will to him as an individual, he just didn't fit with us and who we were deciding to be.

But what is so important about this story is what

happened once we decided to part ways. As great as this employee was, once we let him go, the whole department performed at a higher level. He had once been our top performer, but not long after we had more people match and even surpass him. What I learned as a leader is that once you have established these values, it stops just being a tool to determine who can work for you and who can't, but it becomes a promise to your employees that you are going to surround them with people who also embody these characteristics. They will respond in ways that will surprise you.

I can't stress how much this concept changed our company. It made us go from being a company that was growing, shrinking, growing, and shrinking again as people came and left, to a company that had like-minded people side by side who were all moving in the same direction. We didn't have to hire people just to stick them in a role and have them burn out. Everybody was working towards a common mission.

> **Put your core values as a company before the profit you might make from a high-performing individual.**

It's hard to make those tough decisions because you're grateful for all of your employees and what they have done for your business. But this is what I mean by choosing fit over talent. It means putting your core values as a company before the profit you might make from a high-performing individual. And in the end, we actually became more profitable by getting rid of that individual because it allowed everyone else to step up. He had been standing on their backs. Instead of lifting his colleagues up, he was stepping on them to get to where he was. Once we made that tough decision and saw the success that came as a result, we realized our whole company needed to be that way. We needed to stop protecting the prima donnas and we needed to start living the culture that we wanted.

And we've done it. As a result, our business has flourished and continues to flourish. Some people might think this is crazy because as a manager and as a leader, your success is measured most of the time by your profit. But it's a matter of investing in the long-term health and success of your company versus the short-term success.

DON'T MEASURE THE FRUIT

Oftentimes if your business is struggling in some way, that problem can feel enormous and difficult to solve. If you are struggling to hire talent, or not obtaining enough clients, telling your team, "We need to find quality talent," or, "Let's go close some clients," doesn't actually solve the problem at hand.

This is why I believe you have to measure what produces the fruit, not the fruit itself. What I mean by this is that the success of your business is not actually measured in results, but in the methods put in place to achieve those results.

Keeping with the fruit metaphor, whether you have a shortage or an overabundance of fruit, that result is caused by something. You have to look at what actually produced the fruit: the number of seeds you put in the ground, the quality of the soil, and the weather conditions. It's the same in business. If you're not getting new clients, it's not because new clients aren't out there, it's because you didn't do the things you needed to do to earn their business.

What are the granular details of the sales process that gains you clients? Are your rates competitive? Are your salespeople clearly explaining what distinguishes you from the competition? Are you forming a natural rapport with prospective clients? Do you gain their trust through metrics for success? When you can identify the things needed to do to earn their business and the changes that need to be made in order for that to happen, the problem becomes much more manageable.

The same thought process applies to your employees. Your focus should not be on the fruit itself, but the people doing the planting. Do you have your core values clearly stated? Do all of your employees reflect these core values? Are these values present in how your employees conduct business? Your results will be better when you can ensure your employees are representing these values in every facet of their work. Ultimately, you will find that these problems occur less and less when you have employees that consistently embody your core values because they are the ones producing the fruit.

CHAPTER 7

HOW TO KEEP TALENT

In this day and age, employees expect to look for new jobs multiple times in their life. The days of working for a single company for the entirety of your career are, for the most part, over. Now, call me old-fashioned, but this is still something I strive for. I want to engage in a relationship with my employees that lasts a lifetime. I want them not only to stay, but to be happy and content in their decision to stay.

If my employees can answer yes to the Four Fundamentals, they will have everything they need to stay with my company. If they can answer yes to those four questions, and they still find a better opportunity, I can be content in knowing I helped them on their journey and be proud of their success. There are a number of systems I put in place to make sure my employees have everything they need professionally, emotionally, and mentally.

I have implemented a series of written repeatables and measurables to ensure my employees know what great looks like. I have created a system where their managers and colleagues can check on them and know what is happening in their lives. And perhaps most importantly, I listen to them and take their advice into account. By doing so, I tie their individual success to the success of the company. I encourage them to share their thoughts and ideas, so they want to stay on in order to see their ideas implemented and the company thrive.

CONVINCE THEM THEY'RE NOT SMALL

When my children were kids they played volleyball, and they played on some travel teams. We would go to tournaments where there would be 8,000 girls playing volleyball. There was always a team there from Puerto Rico. If you ever watch volleyball on TV, the girls are averaging 6 feet tall; some of them are 6'6 or 6'7. There's usually one position on a team that's a shorter person or an amazing athlete that can jump four feet in the air, and they become a hitter. But when we would go to these tournaments, there was always a team from Puerto Rico that would either win or be in the top two or three, and they were always really short people, all of them.

I used to think to myself, "Whoever's coaching that team gets it. Because they convinced those players that they're not small."

I ended up speaking to the coach.

He had a philosophy. He said, "We don't let anything touch the floor on our side of the net. That's our rule."

And if you think about it, in volleyball, it's simple. In order to score a point, the ball is either going to hit off somebody's hands, go out of bounds, or it's going to touch the floor on their side. The way I understand the coach's success in that situation is he took the time to identify what great looks like. For him and his players, great is not letting the ball touch the floor. He communicated that vision clearly to them and they believed him. Obviously, they believed him because they won.

It would have been so easy for those players to take one look at the competition and get nervous. They could turn to their coach and say, "Those players are 6 feet tall, there is no way we can win!"

But he gave them one simple directive: "The ball doesn't touch the floor on our side of the net." He convinced them they weren't small and made that directive achievable.

In business, I want to do the exact same thing. I want to give my employees clear measurables for what success looks like, and I want to make them believe they can achieve those measurables. This means giving my employees the relevant training to ensure they succeed; it means fostering a positive work culture in which they can turn to their colleagues for support and encouragement; it means empowering them to speak up and play an active role in the direction of our company.

Yes, those players had one simple rule by which they could understand success, but they also had a coach that made sure they knew that success was attainable, no matter their height. Good managers do the same thing. They show employees what great looks like, and they make sure employees know that greatness can be achieved.

WRITTEN REPEATABLES

I often get asked about employee involvement in my business. How do you engage your employees? And we will get into the written repeatable process, the step-by-step way we do that. But I'd like to talk about the scenario that helped start us on this path.

Years ago, I had a used car store. I had a vendor that sold these little magazines that you list your cars for sale in. One day he came to me and said, "John, can I borrow you for two minutes?"

"Sure."

He said, "Listen, is it my job to bring you prospects? Or is it my job to sell the product?"

"Well, I think it's your job to... " Of course, it's

both, but kiddingly, I said, "No, it's your job to bring them to us, and then we're supposed to do the work."

"Well, one of your stores that I'm doing the best for is firing me, and the problem isn't my ability to get them prospects, it's what they do with them when they get them."

I said, "Okay."

He said, "They do call recording. Can we take three minutes and just listen to some of the calls?"

I said, "Sure, let's do it."

We sat down, and we listened to these people answering the phone. I'll give you an example:

A customer called in and said, "Hey, I'm interested in said vehicle."

The person who worked for me at the time said, "That vehicle is already gone."

He said, "Oh, really? Do you have anything else like it?"

He said, "No, that was the only one, but if you keep checking back with us we should get some more in. Thank you."

Click. And that was the call. In our business, that's as bad as it could possibly get, other than cussing out the customer. I listened, and he played me two or three examples that were just atrocious.

I made the decision the next day that I was going to go in and phone train. I start training, and I'm going through my normal process, just like I have for years. We get to the place where we're going to test call some of our employees to see how they do, including some of our tenured employees that have been with us for a long time, and everybody says, "Call Ken."

Ken was one of my managers at the time. He was probably one of the best teachers in the company. We called Ken, and we had him go through this process that we follow, and he did a great job. He was articulate, he served in the call, he did a lot of things. The problem was what he did was completely different from what I was teaching. And that told me something. I realized, "Okay, I have got to go back to the drawing board, and I've got to put a written repeatable process in place."

This was where written repeatable processes became so important in our organization. When my company was small, I was the teacher. Everybody was following my lead on how to do things. But as we grew and we hired people from other organizations, the methods began to diverge. Their methods were good, but they were different from what I taught, and that inconsistency became a problem.

You find this in a lot of businesses. If it's a construction company, your employees build houses with one company, and then they go to another company, and now they're at your company. And although this person may be great, and their way works well, if it isn't your company's specific way of doing things, it creates a confusing message for your employees. Because what they see is one manager is telling them one thing, and another manager is telling them another.

I pulled my team together, and I said, "Let's design our way. Let's take the time to map out what we all agree is the way that we're going to teach from today forward as a group, and every person in our company is going to be taught this way."

We designed this elaborate program on how to handle incoming sales calls. It was really good and pretty consistent with how I had done it. We changed a few things, but not a lot. But before we were going to stamp it in stone and make it law, we had to test the theory. We brought some of our staff in and said, "Listen, here are our thoughts. As a company, we're going to implement a written repeatable process, so our training messages are the same. This is our new script; we'd love to get your opinion on it."

I went right in as an example for the staff. Now, back in the day when I was a salesman, price was the most important thing. Everybody that called in wanted to know, "What's your best price? And what's my car worth?" That was how I answered the mock calls.

One of the younger salespeople in the room raised his hand and said, "Excuse me, Mr. Hiester?"

I said, "Yes, sir?"

He said, "You know, people don't ask those questions anymore."

"What?"

He said, "Yeah, when they're calling in, they want to know if the vehicle is here, and is it like you represented it online?"

What had happened was customers had gone on the internet and found the cheapest vehicle, but it was already sold, or when they got there, it wasn't as the company represented it. The most important thing to them was, "Do you have it? Is it equipped like you said, and will it be there when I get to the store?"

Whether you realize it or not, your industry is constantly evolving. Whether you're in the medical business or advertising business, it doesn't matter. What worked last year or 10 years ago may work only on some level today. But taking the time to identify how things have changed and changing your system accordingly is going to make a tremendous difference. It may only need a minor tweak here and there to appeal to today's evolving market. It may require an entire restructuring. Either way, your business will benefit. And even if what you were doing worked well before, you will find the new system to be even more effective.

I listened to this employee, and I got a consensus from the room. I said, "What you're saying is the most important thing customers want to know is if it's here? Is it equipped like you represent it to be, and will it be there if I come to look at it?"

This was a complete dynamic shift in our business. I go to what they call a 20 group, where we meet with 20 like-sized businesses and we compare notes on how we do things. When I presented this idea that I'm about to share with you in this group, they laughed at me. In fact, one of the guys heckled me and made fun of me for my idea. And, of course, he's out of business now, and we're 300 times bigger than we were then.

Our idea was this, and it may seem small but in the car dealership world, it was a big deal. We said, "Okay, when a person calls in, the most important thing to them is, 'Is it available? Is it like you represented it, and will it be there when I get there?' What if we started holding cars for people to come look at them?"

In this 20 group, there was a guy that was talking about how important it is that we're transparent in our business and love our customers. Yet it occurred to me, we're going to tell a customer that we have a car, and by the time they get here, it will have been sold to somebody else? That's not demonstrating love, and that's not transparent, in my opinion.

I shared the idea with the 20 group. "What if, when a customer asks us if a car is available, we say, 'Hey, let me check and see if it's here and available.' When I come back to the phone, either it's available or it's not. And if it is available, we say, "Hey, great news the car you wanted is available. Would you like us to place it on hold so you can come and take a look at it?"

People laughed at the idea, but by implementing this policy we were addressing a need the customer had. The customer's response is always, "You'll do that?"

And we say, "Absolutely. What time can you be here?" We schedule an appointment for them to come see the car. If they can't be here in a timely fashion, we say, "It's no problem. Can we bring the car to you?"

I think in many ways, keeping talented employees boils down to the same thing that keeps customers. That is simply being attentive to their needs and responding accordingly. If you are as attentive to the needs of your employees as you are to your customers, you won't have any trouble keeping talent. This directly relates back to one of the Four Fundamentals of our business: Do I have a voice? Do my employees feel empowered to speak up on issues that concern them? I think about that employee who made that statement about customers wanting to know if we had the vehicle.

Most employees would have been scared to go to the owner of the company and say, "Hey, you're wrong, man. What you're saying, nobody even cares about anymore." That's a hard statement, but he was doing it with a pure heart. And because of it, I had the utmost respect for him. I was grateful, because if he hadn't said that, we wouldn't have changed our business model. I know if I never do any of the things my employees suggest, they'll stop suggesting. If I belittle them when they come up with ideas, they'll stop coming up with ideas. Does what I do matter? Do I have a voice? These are the foundational principles by which I run my business and take care of my employees. I never want my employees to feel like they can't make a suggestion because nobody will listen to them. If that ever becomes part of the culture of my business, then I have failed.

We listened to him, and we designed this program. Two years later, one of the manufacturers we work with came out with training for phone scripts, so if you entered an agreement with one of their vendors, they'd

> *My success as a businessman comes from how well my company performs. But the success of my company comes from how empowered my employees are.*

pay for some of the support. One of the vendors came to our store and watched how we did things. They were one of the top phone training companies in the industry, and they looked at our conversion rate on appointments, and it was 10 points higher than their average dealer. They asked to use our process so that they could sell it to other dealerships. My success as a businessman comes from how well my company performs. But the success of my company comes from how empowered my employees are.

LOOK IN THEIR EYES

Being attentive to the needs of your employees is a learning process like anything else. There is a story that really illustrated this for me: I was at a meeting in Greensboro, North Carolina, and the speaker said, "Hey, I just want to let you know the smartest guy in the car business is here today with us," and he looked over at my table.

Of course, I did a little chest bow and sat back in my seat like he was talking about me, even though I knew that he wasn't. But the guy that he was talking about was sitting next to me, and he ran one of the most profitable dealerships in a large automotive group chain. I had the fortune of sitting next to him, so, of course, what are you going to do? I picked his brain. I asked him, "What makes you the smartest guy in the car business?"

He said, "I'm not the smartest guy in the car business. We've got some things that we do that make our business very successful."

I said, "Man, I'd love to come by and see it sometime."

He said, "Look, anytime."

"Well, can we come when we leave here?"

I took three of my team members with me because they were at the meeting too. We went to his business, and what he did was pretty simple.

He said, "I'm the general manager, so I'm over the whole company." Every dealership has multiple businesses within it. They have a parts business, they have a service business, some of them have body shops, they have a sales operation, they have a finance operation, and, of course, accounting. As a general manager, you have a person that leads each of those departments that reports to you. What he said was, "I have a series of metrics that I look at every day from my employees that tell me whether they're on track or off track. And really what I'm doing is I'm looking at the metrics, and I'm looking in their eyes, and I'm seeing, are they ready to win the game?"

I like to think about this in relation to coaching. What makes a great coach? You certainly have to be a good recruiter, you make the players build trust in the vision, and you're a great communicator. All of these things make a great coach. Well, the same things apply for management, except one of the qualities that I would apply is that when they get the team ready to play, they get the team ready to win. If the team's losing halfway through the game, they have a half-time speech that gets them to understand why they're in the position they're in and what they're going to do differently in the second half to ensure that they win. If you liken it to sports, that's the way that works.

Well, let me tell you something. Professional sports and professional business are exactly the same. You want to recruit the best players, you want to recruit players that work well together, and you want to motivate them to do more and accomplish more. What this guy did was he met with his staff every morning and he had six questions per person that told him whether they were on track and headed in the right direction, or they weren't. And if they weren't, then he knew he'd better go spend time in that department that day. If they were, then he'd meet with the fixed operations, and he'd go to lunch with somebody. He'd celebrate. That's what you hope to do every day.

How do you translate that into what we're talking about? Well, I hope that every position that you hire has a leader who is responsible for that person's success. And that person has to have a clear path of what success looks like. They have to have clear standards they are going to be measured against. And we need to make sure that, mentally, they are prepared to win the game today.

How do you make sure? It's simple. You look in their eyes, and you listen to their voice every single day. Obviously, I have over 300 employees. I'm not able to listen to every person in my business. I'm not able to look in the eyes of every person in my business, but hopefully, the person that they report to can. This is why most great leadership books or programs advise breaking teams into fewer than nine people. When you have over nine people, it becomes hard to effectively impact those people.

I hear a lot of talk from people who have big companies and manage a lot of employees. But in my mind, if that team is bigger than 11 people, there should be somebody else involved with leading that team. They don't necessarily have to have a manager title, but they have to be a team leader; they need to be acting in the bosses' stead. There's a reason that football teams and basketball teams put team captains in place: It's because the coaches recognize that there needs to be somebody holding the players accountable because if the team is big enough, you know one person can't manage 60 people effectively. The idea is that somebody has to be in your life who can maintain your vision among your employees, who can enforce those core values

I met with one of my managers last week. This woman was the most reluctant when it came to the system we use to manage our business. She fought it for a long time. Part of this system is daily huddles, just five minutes at the start of each day to look in the eyes of the team and determine if they are engaged or not. It quickly became apparent that this method was working. People were happy, and we could tell every day that they were happy. I had a conversation with her, and despite the reservations she had, she told me this:

"The thing that's working the best for my team is the daily huddle. It's quick, it's five minutes, we get together. If there's a problem, we address the problem. If we've got stuff we have to accomplish today, we set the stage, and everybody's on the same page. Break and go." If you think about a huddle the way it is used in football, that's exactly what it is. It's a team gathering together to say, "Okay, here's the play we're running. Let's make sure everybody's on the same page." This way we can hold each other accountable, and we can celebrate each other's victories; that's why that huddle exists. And even if she wasn't initially enthusiastic about it, she couldn't deny how effective it was, and she came to appreciate it.

We have designed our company in such a way that our managers can look in the eyes of their employees every single day. I look into the eyes of my group of team leaders, they look into the eyes of their team, and so on and so forth. That is how we know every single person in our company is in a great place. And if they're not, we are working to get them back to that place. We serve them where they are.

How do we do that? Sometimes it is just sitting down with a cup of coffee. Sometimes an employee has lost sight of the vision and needs to be reminded by the people they work with. I always know where the company is going to be a year from now, but as time goes on, we need to update employees on progress and direction. Most of the time they only see what is directly in front of them, but they also need to be included in the larger vision.

This system is in place to keep all of our employees refreshed. My expectation is that someone is looking into the eyes of every employee every morning and knowing where their heart is. That is how we know we are winning. We are constantly making sure our employees are engaged and not distracted by something going on in the company or in their personal lives.

This man who I sat next to at the event I mentioned before was brilliant. He said, "I'm not really looking to see if they're doing their job or not. I'm looking to see if they're ready to do their job. When I look into their eyes in the morning, if there's a problem, there's no better time for me to get it out than today. And we need to figure it out. Is it that their kid is in the hospital, is it that their dog died, is it that they're broke? What is it? Maybe I can help, maybe I can't, but most of the time, caring enough to listen and work through it is enough to get them out of their funk and get them on track to win this game with you."

This inspired me because let me tell you something: In sports, if you're not ready to play the game, that's when the major upsets happen. The team isn't ready. And you need to approach your business with so much passion that not one day is going to go by where the team is not prepared to win. That's the difference. That's why a coach can go from one team to another, take the team that was losing and make them National Champions. They do this by selling them on the vision, communicating what they're going to do, communicating how they're going to do it, and showing love and passion for seeing their players be the best that they can be.

IS YOUR HEAD IN THE GAME?

We were amazed at how the practices this man used in his daily huddles aligned with our own weekly department meetings. We had implemented these meetings from Gino Wickman's *Traction*. The goal of these meetings is to work on the business rather than in the business. They are structured in such a way that we get to learn more about our employees.

The meeting goes like this: It starts out where we share something positive that happened in our work life and in our personal life in the last week. The reason we do this is that we want to be a team. We want to make sure that the rest of our employees know how much they mean to us as a company and to each other. We also really push our employees for details about their lives. If they share a story about their son, we ask what his name is. What you find when you ask these questions is that you create a culture where you can walk down the hall and bump into somebody, and they'll ask you, "Hey, how's Jeremy doing? Did your kid end up pitching a no-hitter? I heard he was doing really well."

Whatever the personal information is, our employees become a part of each other's lives. I believe that is one of the biggest strengths that we have as a company. And this comes back to the Four Fundamentals again and again: Does what I do matter? Do I have a voice? Am I growing? Am I fairly compensated? The first three really come into play when you talk about the overarching mission for the company. From a cultural standpoint, we have made leaps and bounds in terms of getting our employees to know each other, to interact with each other, and to share a common vision.

When we go into these meetings, we start with those prompts about something positive in the employees' professional and personal lives because we want to know, we want to be in their lives. Even though the manager runs the meeting, it's not their meeting. The goal isn't for the facilitator to tell everyone what to do, but to look into their eyes and minds, so that once a week the managers can check in and find out if their head is in the game.

If somebody can't come up with something positive to say that's happening in their work week or their personal life, then they have an issue. Our managers can recognize that that's a pathway to a bad situation. As a result, sometime soon the manager will have to sit down with that employee and love them enough to make sure they know how important they are. And we apply this philosophy not only to individual employees, but to departments as a whole.

When I sense that something is not on track in a department or in the business, I start my investigation by meeting with people within that department and just having conversations with them. I'll sit them down, and I'll say, "Hey, look, how is everything going?" It's that simple, just having a true and personal conversation.

IDENTIFY A PROBLEM, BUILD A SOLUTION

Earlier in this book, I have covered the critical questions I ask my employees:

- If there's anything you could change, what would you change about the way we do business?
- If you could clone three people to dominate the industry, who would those three people be?

The idea of this exercise is to get my employees to think about who they admire within the company. Having this information tells me where their heart is regarding the people they work with. If somebody is on that list or somebody was on that list and is not anymore, there is obviously a reason.

Sometimes an employee won't appear on that list, and I'll ask, "What about so and so?" This allows me to have a better understanding of what is going on with that particular employee. I am also especially looking to see if some of the leadership is on that list, because I'm hoping that they're inspiring their employees.

Also, I ask, "If you were to dominate the industry, who would be the last person you would take?"

Well, I had an employee who was a Finance Manager, and we have specific ways we measure their success. This person had been successful in the metrics for the most part, but when I looked at the company as a whole, I found we were leaving that person behind. Where three years ago he had constantly been in the top two or three in the company, he had now fallen to the middle of the pack or below average. Even though he was hitting the measurables that we had put in place for him, he had fallen down in the rankings consistently.

When I had this conversation with those employees, he showed up on the last-to-take list twice, where he used to be the first pick for people I would clone. I knew that this was not just a poor employee; he was very intelligent, arguably one of the smartest people in the company. But I knew from where he was appearing on his colleague's lists that he was having an issue.

The metrics were dropping, and people were noticing. I asked why, and they said it was because he was not engaged. He had a bad attitude. Even though this person didn't report directly to me, I didn't feel like what was happening could wait.

I called this person to my office, and I said, "Listen, we need to have a conversation. You know I have the utmost respect for you and your ability to do this job. Unfortunately, when I'm looking at the metrics, you're dropping down in the rankings." I turned them around and showed him. "Here is your performance, here is everybody else's numbers, you're this far off. But what concerns me," I said, "Is that I talked to six different people and asked them who they would clone, and three years ago, you would have been on almost every list. Today you're only on one. And when I asked the question, who's the last person you would pick, you showed up on three of those lists."

I had to be honest with him. "Quite frankly, you showed up because pretty much everybody is saying you're being an ass, and that is unacceptable. Our core values are what we use to decide who can come here, but it's also a promise that I made to everybody that works here. I made a promise that I'm going to surround them with people who embody these core values, that are going to have a servant attitude, that are going to love people, that are going to be professional in the way they do things. They're going to have a get-it-done attitude, and they are going to have character and integrity."

Because I knew this employee, I knew he had character and integrity. That was never a question. But I had to tell him, "The truth is that you are struggling to embody the servant mentality and loving everybody. I can live with your metrics being off, we can work on that together, but I can't change this. Only you can and you need to decide whether you're going to change it, or we have to figure out another path."

He looked at me and he said, "Well, look, John, the metrics, we could work on. The other one I can fix. If I'm being an ass or if people are feeling this way, I can fix that."

This was an incredibly difficult moment. In my heart, I was afraid we had gone too far without loving this guy. We had failed at holding him accountable and we let some behaviors happen that should not have happened. I was really concerned. But I can tell you that fast-forward to last week, I did the same exercise with six people, and he showed up on four of the lists as the first person they would clone, and he didn't show up on anybody's last list.

I very rarely ever see a turnaround in only a month or two, but all his colleagues say he is completely different. He was staying out of meetings, now he's in the meetings, he's participating, he's teaching, he's helping. He did a 180-degree flip. Now, I'm not suggesting that you let employees get to the stage that he did. I think you owe it to them to love them earlier and let them know that you're seeing a negative pattern in their behavior. He's a success story, but it just goes to show how you can allow people to enter a habit where they are not performing without even realizing they are there. Pay attention to what the metrics are telling you. They all tell a story. This guy loves this business. He'd tell you he plans on retiring with us. He wants to be here forever. He just lost his way. But I'm grateful that our metrics and my philosophy allow us to correct someone who is a valuable member of our team, rather than losing talent because he wasn't where he needed to be.

The best way to keep and maintain talent is to fix yourself first. Because as easy as it would be to point the finger at him and analyze how he became an ass, it's not really about that. It's about his boss, the layer between me and him that allowed him to get to the point where his performance was suffering. I know he's one of those guys that's super at what he does. You can count on him for anything, and you know that he's going to give it 110%. Because these kinds of employees are so reliable, you kind of shove them to the side and take their performance for granted. When he screwed up, I know he didn't screw up. His direct manager and I did. Because we let him get to that point.

SIX HEATS

There is an old business story that has really inspired my philosophy and directly relates to the case of this employee. And that is the story of Charles Schwab, the eventual President of Carnegie and Bethlehem Steel. At the time, Carnegie Steel was one of the larger steel companies in the U.S. The story goes that Charles Schwab had a steel mill that was not performing; the metrics were off. They had to make a decision about what would happen to the plant. They were in a meeting, and they were going to decide whether they should close that plant or keep it open. Charles Schwab said, "Well, listen, I'm going to go there and I'm going to check it out before we make a decision."

When they looked at the performance of the mill, it was one of the least performing mills in their whole fleet. Charles Schwab traveled there, he went into the business, and nobody knew he was coming. You can imagine how the employees were all on edge. But he didn't call a meeting, he just went in, said hello to everybody, and walked around the plant and observed.

The first thing he looked for was, do they have quality employees? He saw that they really seemed to. People seemed to care. He looked around and looked at the processes. Well, the processes looked like every other steel mill's. There were three shifts and at the end of the first shift, he went up to one of the foremen, and he said, "Hey, how are you? I'm Charles Schwab."

The foreman said, "Oh, I know you are. I'm so and so."

"Listen," Charles Schwab said. "I have one question for you. How many heats did you have on your shift?"

The foreman said, "This will be our sixth, sir. We will have six heats."

A heat is what fires the furnace. In a steel mill, every time they fire the furnace, the steel melts and pours into the ingots to make the product that they sell. Charles Schwab understood that the simplest measure, the more times that steel mill fired that furnace, the more money they were going to make as a company.

He said, "Great job, thank you." He left the foreman and went to the breakroom. This was a long time ago, so they had time punches where the employees punched their timecards. Charles Schwab went to the breakroom where everybody came in and out and he took a big piece of chalk. He wrote a giant six on the floor and left.

Naturally, all the employees were excited and wanted to know what had happened. They were all buzzing around asking, "What did Charles Schwab want? What did he say to that foreman?" Finally, they asked the foreman.

He said, "Well, he just asked me how many heats we had."

And the employees asked, "What'd you tell him?"

"Six."

The employees were trying to puzzle it out. Imagine the CEO of your company coming in, drawing a six on the floor, and then leaving. You would want to know what was going on. It didn't take long before they realized what the six meant.

They went to punch out, and the next shift was coming to punch in, and there was this giant six on the floor. The employees for the next shift asked, "What's with the six? Why the six?"

The employees from the previous shift told them, "Charles Schwab came in and wrote it on the floor. That's how many heats we had on our shift." Well, you can bet that now the next shift was going to fire

> *I have got to figure out what allows my employees to thrive in their department. What tangible thing can they control that contributes to the success of this business?*

the furnace a minimum of six times, but more likely seven or more. They didn't want to be outdone.

This went on until they had 10 or 12 heats at one point. That plant ended up being the most successful steel mill in their whole operation, so the story goes. The point of this story is, as a business, you have got to figure out what produces your steel.

It's not about how much steel you have, it's about how you get there. Your business is not about your amount of product, but what produces the product. When you start thinking about your product, if you can increase the speed at which you make it, and the efficiency you make it with, you can sell a lot more.

What I learned from that is in my business, I have got to figure out what allows my employees to thrive in their department. What tangible thing can they control that contributes to the success of this business?

What Charles Schwab's employees understood is, "We can figure out how to fire that furnace more." They understood what great looks like.

CREATE MEASURABLES

The same way Schwab's employees discovered what they could do to make the mill more successful, my employee figured out what he could do to make his performance more successful. He said, "I can figure out how to fix my attitude." That was within his control the whole time. He realized that by changing his behavior, he could also change the opinions of the people around him. He could let them see him contribute, he could get involved in meetings, he could train, he could make an effort. That way his colleagues felt like he was serving them. It's not just about your greed or getting what you want out of the situation, it's about you putting in the time and effort. And his team understood that.

Imagine the possibilities if you could take every single position at your company and break it down to each individual responsibility. Ask yourself what each individual in each role could do to play their part more efficiently. In order to do that, you also need to know those individuals, love them, and honor them as people.

An important part of that is that you are communicating to your employees what great looks like in their position and how it contributes to the success of the company. Sometimes we get so focused on the former, that we forget about the latter. Employees need to know why their work matters. You need to understand not only how each position functions, but how it contributes to the larger goal; the measurables you gauge them on should support that larger goal.

I recently met with a guy who was interviewing for a promotion. I sat down with him and went through the responsibilities that I felt were most important to him succeeding at this job. I explained to him, "Look, I want you to understand why I am here. I am here because in the position you were in before, you weren't managing people. Even though you were managing a department, you weren't responsible for

the success of the people that came into this organization. I want to make sure that you understand
what I expect of this position." I went through all the
core values and the specific steps of what is expected
in this position. I even told him what my concerns
were about him filling this role.

Finally, he said, "John, thank you for doing this.
It makes me realize why this job needs to be done
this way."

When I hire someone, I am thinking about their
success long-term. Long-term success means the
employee needs to understand not only how something is done, but why. Our way of doing things isn't
the best or only way, but within our company, it has
to be consistent. If our way of doing things is going
to change, we all have to change.

When I first read *Traction* by Gino Wickman
and started adopting the Entrepreneurial Operat-
ing System (EOS) into our company, I realized there
were a lot of positions that I didn't fully understand.
I would look at a department like accounting and ask
myself, "How on Earth do I implement measurables
for the work these people do?" But the truth is, when
you really break it down, they're the easiest to put
measurables on.

They have measurables that they're responsible for, and those things are keeping our accounts
receivable below a small number, which helps our
cash flow, which gives us the ability to buy more, do
more, operate more, and be more efficient in the way

we do things. Now we have more negotiating power, and we can borrow money cheaper. Their job does impact the way the whole company functions.

Before instituting EOS, our company was fragmented in our direction. Everybody was responsible for a variety of tasks. What we found by separating them and making one person responsible for a singular task, was an increase in accountability and that task being accomplished more efficiently. This doesn't mean that others can't help them with it, but it means that they bear the responsibility for the completion of that one task.

This allows your employees to have focused energy and responsibility for that task. What we realized from our measurables was that the way we had originally done it was preventing our employees from succeeding at anything. Each employee had so much on their plate they couldn't succeed at any one thing.

For example, in the accounting office, they handle payables, receivables, title-work, account restructuring, and account balances. There are all these different responsibilities in that one department. We assigned one person to each task and made them accountable for it. It doesn't mean they can't help with other things, but they are accountable to their task. The success of their task is

> *If more than one person is responsible for a task, no one is responsible.*

on them and only them. If more than one person is responsible for a task, no one is responsible. We have seen so much success in our departments, especially accounting, since we incorporated this process.

The problem is many companies don't take the time to help their employees understand how important their role is. If you treat your employees as if the success of the business does not depend on them, they will come to believe it, and their work will reflect it.

> **If you treat your employees as if the success of the business does not depend on them, they will come to believe it, and their work will reflect it.**

But if you could take the time to understand every single position within your company, as I have in mine, you can identify and put in place metrics that allow your employees not only to succeed, but to know they are succeeding.

You must have metrics. We truly believe that measurables free people, not restrict them. Every employee in our business has three to five measurables they are beholden to. If you're constantly trying to figure out what your boss wants from you, you can't be an independent thinker, and you can't think outside the box. If you are constantly going from one task to the next trying to figure out what is most important, it creates anxiety and wastes time. By understanding what great looks like, you can finish what is most important. This frees up your time and your mind so you can think about other things. Some people say, "Well, that's micromanaging." I believe it is the complete opposite. It's liberated management.

We also have quarterly responsibilities that move us closer to our annual goal. In Gino Wickman's *Traction*, these are called "Rocks." We have a goal we want to accomplish. We set it through what is called a Vision Traction Organizer. The Vision Traction Organizer tells us what our big goals are for 10 years out, or 3 years out, or 1 year out. We've made a decision that in order to achieve that big goal this year, we need to accomplish these things.

This method is based on the theory that if you're going to fill a glass with rocks, sand, and water, you've got to do it in the right order, or it won't fit in the glass. Rocks are quarterly things that we've established are the most important for this quarter to move us towards that annual goal. Most people have one or two rocks in addition to their three to five measurables. This is how we articulate to our employees what they can do to succeed on a day-to-day basis, but also how we articulate how that work fits into our long-term goals.

Here's your job that we've hired you for, these are the things that you have to get done and focus on, this is what we're going to measure. Well, if I'm an employee working for you and I know exactly how you're going to measure me, when I get to your measurement, I'm free to think outside the box. It also eliminates doubt and anxieties employees may have about their performance. Metrics allow employees to know that they are doing well. They allow your employees to see what great looks like and to know their greatness is crucial to the greatness of the company.

How do you inspire somebody? You make it clear what you expect. You communicate it clearly. You draw a picture of what great looks like, and then most importantly, you hold them accountable for that and praise them for their success.

LISTEN TO YOUR EMPLOYEES

My daughter Ashley had her first quarterly meeting with her staff a few weeks ago. This is something she has directly pulled from my business practice, and you will see more of this as the story progresses.

She called me one day and said, "Look, Dad, we're having a quarterly meeting. Can you walk me through what you do in your meetings so that I can practice and be ready for mine?"

"Yeah, absolutely, let's do it," I said. We did, and I was even present at the meeting itself, just listening in. The first thing I noticed is the diversity of her employees. She has part-time college students, she has chefs, she has baristas. There is a wide variety of personalities and career experiences. I, of course, was looking at it from the standpoint of my business.

We've got salespeople, management, and all kinds of employees, and you'd think these people are used to going to meetings and doing stuff like that.

But one thing I've learned is that no matter what your business is, you will have people who either care about the company or people who care about the check. I sat in her meeting, and she ran the whole thing. This should be familiar to you by now: The first thing she did was ask them one positive thing about their personal life and one positive about their work that happened in the last week.

They all shared and seemed very engaged. At one point, they got into discussing whatever issues they were having. She wrote down a list of all the issues they were facing and then asked, "What are some things that if we did it differently would drastically improve our business?" Every employee in the room started contributing. She had them go around the room and share their ideas for things that could be done to improve the business until there was a huge list of about 30 items. Finally, she said, "Okay, let's vote on three of them. Which ones do you think would have the largest impact on our business?" She had them do this part individually, privately writing down their top three. And once the votes were compiled, the ones with the most votes were the ones her team began to work on solving.

One part that really impacted me during this was one of her chefs. It's important to note that this man is a veteran of the industry; he's been a chef for 17 years. He asked, "Can I say something?"

She said, "Sure."

"I've worked in restaurants for 17 years," he said. "I have never been in a meeting where leadership cared about our opinion on how to better the business. I'm just so proud to be a part of this. And I think it's so awesome that you're considering what we think. The fact that you obviously care, makes me care."

I was so moved because he was the last person in the room I would have expected to come out and say, "I'm glad to have a meeting." It was clear he had a big heart, and he was in it for the company, not just for the paycheck.

There are lots of different tricks and stories in this chapter that will help you keep talent. But the most important thing I would say is that whatever your business might be, never lose sight of how important it is to your staff to be considered. Never lose sight of those first two fundamentals for employee engagement:

- **Do I matter?**
- **Do I have a voice?**

It is critical you consider what they think, because their ideas and their thoughts may be what builds your business into the great company it can become. I can't stress this enough, and it doesn't matter what they do. Everybody should feel important in their job, from the head chef to the dishwasher. If someone comes along and tries to offer your employee twice what they are making with you, it will be this principle that makes them say, "No thanks. I love where I'm at, I love what I do. I'm a part of something."

This is especially relevant at the time I am writing this because of the COVID-19 pandemic. People are hesitant to go back to work because they have extra income coming from the government. The truth is, if I was a stay-at-home parent and I'm paying a day-care $1,000 a month, and I'm only making $2,000 a month, and I've got $1,000 coming in from the government, I would probably stay home too. But when you create an environment where your employees know they are cared for, they are heard, and they are protected, you would be surprised what they will do in order to make sure they can come into work each day.

This is happening all over the country. But Ashley has just hired three wonderful new employees as the business continues to grow. I've learned a lot from her business, and I love the approach she's taking. It is because of the way she's approaching the business that her staff is doubling and tripling in size. Now she's facing different decisions like, "How do we get more room? Can we rent more from the plaza? Do we need to add a second location that has a huge kitchen because we've got so much demand?" Truly wonderful problems to have.

I feel that when you take care of your employees, they are going to want to make your business a success. I don't only mean taking care of them monetarily but through the Four Fundamentals of Employee Engagement. When your people feel like they have a voice and they feel like their work matters, they feel like they're growing at some level just by being a part of it, the customers are going to feel it too, and they're going to want to come back and support your business.

Think about it. If you're an employee working for a restaurant and your boss is treating you like crap and you just want to go home, you're not trying to get to know the customers. You might even end up being accidentally rude to customers because you're thinking, "I'm just looking for the next gig." But Ashley's staff are meeting customers and remembering their names and what they ordered. They welcome them when they come into the room. They come to their table and try to go above and beyond because they care about their business. The chef is trying to figure out new recipes to push the boundaries creatively. They wouldn't be doing that if they didn't feel like they were a part of something.

> *Employees who are bought in, who are part of your community, will make a positive difference.*

You're reading this book, and you may be a roofer, you may be a construction worker, you may be an IT company. It's exactly the same. No matter what it is you do. Employees who are bought in, who are part of your community, will make a positive difference. Checked out employees who are thinking about moving on to the next job will make a negative difference.

MY INTERPRETATION OF THE DEMING THEORY

Another classic story that directly relates to this principle is about Edward Deming. Deming was an engineer trying to sell American businesses on world-class manufacturing, and back in those days, our manufacturing companies were making a lot of money, even though their process allowed for significant defective products and waste.

They teach The Deming Theory in business schools now because it was so influential. At the time, for example, a steel manufacturer would produce X number of products, and 75% of it would be good, and 25% would be thrown away. They were making so much money off the 75% that they didn't care, they just continued throwing the 25% away.

Deming's theory was to empower employees to look for mistakes. He told the manufacturers, "Listen, you need your people to stop the assembly line when there's an imperfection, figure out what caused the imperfection, and fix it. That way you can produce 100% good product." He said, "It'll slow you down at first, but eventually you'll have a 100% quality product, and you won't have to worry about flaws getting through or throwing away 25% of what you do."

The greed was so great that at the time, most manufacturers said no. "No, no, no, we don't have time. We're not going to stop our assembly lines. If you stop the assembly line, you're fired." Deming said, "Empower your people to stop when they see an imperfection. Let's get to the bottom of it right now, and let's fix the problem so that we're producing 100% good product." And, of course, nobody listened to him.

Well, American business said no. World War II happened, and after the United States dropped the atomic bomb on Hiroshima and Nagasaki, Deming was sent to Japan to assist with the 1951 Japanese census. Deming applied world-class principles of manufacturing to his work in Japan, and using his own theories, allowed Japan to become world-class manufacturers.

This is the way I understand Deming's theories and how I apply them to my business: He put people in a position where they felt like they were a part of something, where they had a voice, where what they did mattered, and it wasn't just punching a wire on an assembly line. He made employees a part of ensuring that the product was the best it could be.

It all comes back to engaging employees, having them feel like what they do matters, like they have a voice. And naturally, when you're impacting a company, probably the size of those manufacturing plants at that time, you need to feel like you're growing and you're contributing, so you're actually addressing the more important fundamentals in what you do. The single most important factor in keeping talent is letting your employees know their work is important to the success of the company.

CHAPTER 8

THINK OUTSIDE THE BOSS

In order to attract and hire talented employees, you need to understand what they need. To understand what they need, you need to be alert and aware of the needs of the talent you already possess. Being a strong manager not only means being able to fulfill your specific responsibilities as a leader, but it also means being able to step outside that role and see your business from the perspective of your employees. Only when you do that will you be attuned to what prospective hires are looking for.

This is easier said than done. So often we get occupied by the day-to-day tasks that we have to complete, the assignments we need to delegate, and the roles that need to be filled, that we forget to consider these situations from the perspective of our employees. It could be that we get so busy we forget to fully explain a concept and then get frustrated when our employees don't understand. Or we are so focused on accomplishing a task that we don't realize the employee we have delegated it to is not actually equipped to complete it. All of these situations could have been corrected if we had taken a moment to consider what our employees would need to hear in order to fully grasp a concept. They could have been corrected if you had thought outside of your position as the boss. Before you can anticipate and meet the needs of prospective hires, you need to understand the mindset of the people who already work for you. And through doing this, you may find solutions you may never have considered otherwise.

In most businesses, when a situation arises in which employees aren't accomplishing a task, the boss will simply say, "This is a job requirement, do it." What many managers don't realize, however, is that this approach only drives employees further away. It doesn't take the time to explain to the employee the importance of their work. Strong managers have the ability to think outside of their position and empathize with their employees. It is through the practice of thinking outside the boss that allows you to get your employees back on track and explain to them why their work matters, while still fostering a strong relationship with them.

I'll give you an example of what this looks like in practice. We have a requirement for our product specialists and salespeople that they contact 20 people a day. I, as manager, understand the importance of these calls, and why it is so critical our employees do them. But over time, my employees saw it as this daunting task that they hate, and more often than not, they don't get it done. My team and I began noticing the calls were not being made, and it left us puzzled. We couldn't figure out why it was so hard for our employees to get it done. We decided to shoot a motivational video for the employees to help them think differently about these calls and understand why they are so important. It only took about 30 minutes to make. I stood in front of the camera and started to speak.

I said, "I want to talk to you about the importance of the 20 phone calls, and I actually want to change the name of the calls today because not everybody understands what I'm looking for. When I was a salesman, I hated cold calls. I hated reaching out to people I didn't know and trying to sell them something. I understand why it is difficult for you; the 20 phone calls would have been really hard for me early on in my career. But what I want you to understand is why it's so important to our company. And the reason it's so important is that our business is built on relationships.

"One of our vendors is American Financial, which has gone through a change in ownership. I think they're probably one of the best vendor relationships we have. But in my mind, as long as the people that I have that relationship with are still there, and still continue to communicate with me the way they do, their partnership is secure. But if they start pulling my people that I have relationships with and stop following up with me the way they do, I'm going somewhere else. The truth is that they may or may not have the best price or the best product, but I value the relationship so much because of the work they put into it, that I feel obligated to continue to do business with them.

"I want to change the name of those 20 phone calls to the 20 relationship extension calls because that really is what you're doing, you're helping extend our relationships. I don't want you to call them and try to sell them something. I just want you to reach out to them and make sure they know through the conversation that we care about them, and if there is anything they need or don't understand, we are here for them.

"There have been moments where I have called up customers or clients to wish them a happy birthday, or happy holiday. This has nothing to do with making the sale, but rather building a meaningful relationship with them. It is more about building the relationship than making the next sale.

"If you have missed your 20 phone calls by a couple of calls it doesn't seem like a big deal. But if we had 20 salespeople in the store who are not communicating with customers, then it certainly is a big missed opportunity. Our company is growing, we're doubling in size constantly. And if you think about doubling in size, let's say we have 20 salespeople and then double it, so we have 40, and then multiply it by the five businesses we have. 5 multiplied by 40 is 200. If that is happening every day, in a single month that is something like 24,000 missed opportunities.

"As a business owner, do I care that you as an individual didn't make your calls? Not really, but I have to. I have to because if you don't and then Brandon doesn't and Jeremy doesn't, that number gets really big, and we've missed an enormous opportunity. I know, as the owner of this business, that this extension of relationships is of the utmost importance to our business. And I need you to see that too. And I ask you, please, make your phone calls."

We sent out the video, and almost immediately I got word from my managers that it was working. They said it changed their life when it comes to those 20 phone calls because now the employees really understand. By thinking outside of the boss mindset, I was able to see what was stopping them from completing the calls. I could empathize with them and allow them to feel understood. But I also was able to make them see the situation from my perspective too. They were able to understand why it is so important. No matter how tedious the task, people will do it if they understand it is important. By meeting that need and explaining to them the impact their work had, I was able to solve a big problem by filming a video in 30 minutes.

MAINTAIN A PROMISE

By now, you have learned all about our core values. You understand the Four Fundamentals of Employee Engagement. You know how to define what great looks like in prospective and current employees. You understand the importance of selling the vision of your company to everyone you meet.

All of these philosophies are critical to hiring who you want. Through these practices, you can create a positive work culture, create an environment that allows people to produce their best work, and create a steady stream of incoming high-performing talent. All these philosophies relate back to a simple idea, but one that is much easier in theory than in practice: thinking outside the boss.

What I mean by thinking outside the boss is essentially thinking like an employee. To many, this may seem counterintuitive. How can you lead people if you are not thinking from a managerial perspective? I would propose the opposite. In order to lead people, you need to think like the people you are leading. **A company's greatest asset will always be its people.** To successfully maintain that asset and attract more talent, you need to think outside of your perspective as the boss and understand and empathize with the ambitions, concerns, wants, and needs of your employees.

When I train my managers, it is absolutely critical that they not only understand the way I think, but that they understand the way the people they oversee think. Nobody comes into a leadership role in our company without me being involved directly in their development. We also utilize a wide range of training videos so our managers can understand exactly how I think and how their employees think. We have a very stringent training portal set up.

> *You need to think outside of your perspective as the boss and understand and empathize with the ambitions, concerns, wants, and needs of your employees.*

It also helps that the majority of our managers and leadership roles come up through the ranks. We tend to mostly promote from within the company. What this does is it allows our managers to build their leadership knowledge on the first-hand experience of being where the people they are now leading are. It is much easier to think outside the boss when for much of your career, you were exactly where your employees are. All of our general managers have fulfilled other positions in the company before they got the role they are in. We very rarely hire outside of the company for a first-level manager.

When we do bring in somebody from the outside, we make it very clear that they will be fired quicker for a core value infraction than a performance issue. It is paramount that our leadership staff understand that the way they treat and interact with their fellow employees is just as important as how they interact with customers. In order for our managers to understand our employees, they need to know our core values are not just a measuring stick, they are a promise. It has become a promise to our employees that the people surrounding them are going to embody our core values. This is what our employees want, and this is the promise our managers and I are responsible for maintaining. If you cannot uphold this promise to our employees, you are going to fail. It is non-negotiable.

> *This is the promise our managers and I are responsible for maintaining. If you cannot uphold this promise to our employees, you are going to fail. It is non-negotiable.*

THE VALUE OF THE POSITION

In the hiring process, once we have designed the position, once we have identified who the right candidate is based on our little checklist of what a great employee would look like, then it comes down to the belief in the position. We have the belief at our company that energy and excitement is contagious. In order for me to attract somebody to a position that I've created in my company or maybe to an existing position, first, I've got to be sold on the value of that position. I need to truly believe that this position is necessary and is making our company better.

For years, there has been an inherent issue in service drives around the country. As our service department got bigger, we found the need to have more people receiving customers as they bring their car in for service. In most dealerships around the country, this person is a service salesperson. The idea is they're going to find whatever is wrong with that customer's car, explain to them what it is, and convince them to have the work done with us as opposed to taking it somewhere else. Certainly, we never want to sell something that is not needed, but we have to convince them that what they need should be done by us and not by some cheaper or independent shop.

For example, let's take a service department that has four people in the lane. Those people's responsibility is to greet the customer, get their car checked out, explain to them the service needs of the vehicle, and then enter into an agreement to have that service provided. Historically, in our business, there are always one or two employees that are really good at explaining and articulating what needs to happen and why they need to do it now. Generally, these employees have really good numbers.

And then there are usually one or two that are really good at the logistical side of communication.

They are great note-takers, they can enter data and send texts and emails, but they might not be so skilled at the sales and negotiating part of the service.

Over years of dealing with this, I looked at it and I saw that you have a certain percentage of customers that are really happy with us, and you have a certain percentage of them that are not. We came up with the idea to change that model, to hire for two different positions. There are salespeople who can explain what needs to be done to the vehicle, and customer advocates whose sole responsibility is to communicate with the customer and ensure their happiness throughout the process. It is the responsibility of the customer advocate to accurately input the data and to communicate with the customer through the process to ensure that all their needs are met and are done so in a timely manner.

Then what we did was we took the employees who were really good at articulating what the car needed and justifying why that customer needed to do it with us and we slid them back. In doing so, we allowed them to focus exclusively on that part of the job. We separated the position. Obviously, this does not completely translate into every industry, but what it did was it made it easy to track the person we wanted for each position. Each person's sole job is the satisfaction of our customers coming into our service line. Instead of hiring somebody that you would call a greeter for the customer, we took the time to design a customer advocate program.

At the time, there were two common indus-try-wide complaints from customers: poor commu-nication throughout the process and promised time. Processes that should have taken 30 minutes were taking two hours. When we designed this new posi-tion, we required the customer advocate to commu-nicate with the customer at certain points through-out the process. Their job was to ensure everything was on track, so that if there were delays of any kind, we could communicate with the customer and make it as easy as possible for them.

When we first began hiring for this position, they had the tendency to slide into the traditional role of the salesperson. They began getting away from communicating with the customer throughout the process. As humans, we tend to go back to what we know. These employees had never seen a customer advocate role in this capacity and didn't understand why it was needed, so they began fulfilling the re-sponsibilities of a salesperson. What it came down to was that we didn't articulate why there needed to be two separate jobs. They didn't understand how important their job was. We designed a video that went just like this:

"If you're watching this video, you've taken a cus-tomer advocate position with one of our dealerships. The reason I'm sharing this video with you today is I want you to understand how important your posi-tion is to our organization. When we designed this position, we found a need within our organization to have the best customer satisfaction that we possibly could, and hopefully, the best in the industry. The way we figured we could do that was by serving the customer in a way that they wanted to be served and communicating with the customer in the way they wanted to be communicated with, through really effective people with warm, loving personalities that demonstrated care right out of the gate.

"We felt like if we could do this, we could provide better service to that customer and accomplish those things. Well, in my way of looking at this, the role that you've taken within our organization is one of the most important roles in our entire business. The reason I believe that is because you see more customers than anybody. Historically, in our industry, price earns the first sale, service earns the second one. It's a lot easier to keep customers than it is to buy them.

"When you look at it that way, whether those customers come back and buy vehicles is squarely in your position's hands. If you make that person feel warm, you make them feel like we care about them, and you communicate with them throughout the process, even if we have bad news for them, even if what we communicate to them is that their car is broken, or we don't have the part, or we can't fix it, whatever it is, if that customer trusts and believes that you care about them and you're going to follow through to make sure that the things that they need done are done, then our business is going to grow and grow and grow. And just like any other business, as this business grows, opportunity grows. I'm glad you took this job and I'm excited about the opportunity for you, and I'm excited about your future with our company."

The important part of this story is that I took the time to become passionate about what the job was. I knew that the best way to get my employees excited about their position was to be excited about it myself, and in doing so, explain to them how important it is. When I'm trying to hire somebody for that job, if they interview for it, they are going to take it. They're going to feel the passion that I have for that position, and they're going to know the importance of it. Right away, we can cross one of the Four Fundamentals off their list: Does what they do matter? It does.

COMPENSATION

Compensating your employees is one of the hardest topics for leadership. The pay has to be competitive for the position that you're looking to fill. If a person is worth $100,000 a year and you are only paying them $40,000, it is going to be very difficult for them to believe in the vision of your company and work towards that vision. Compensation only becomes a factor if you are paying people unfair wages compared to the rest of your industry. If you are paying employees fairly, it removes that question from the Four Fundamentals.

In our industry, we have so many dealers across the country to whom we can compare our rate. We know where the median lies, so compensation in the dealership should represent X percentage of the profit. We make it clear to our employees that when their volume reaches a certain level, they will make this much money. Every position in our company plays a part in our overarching success, so the success of the company benefits the employees. It is in their best interest to help the company succeed.

My staff is some of the best-compensated people in our industry. People see that and assume it is easy to keep them engaged, but it is actually the opposite. All the money in the world won't keep somebody in a job they hate. You have to constantly be aware of what the industry is paying, and you have to keep your salaries competitive. You don't have to be the highest, but you have to be competitive.

The matter doesn't end there though. You need to remain engaged with your employee throughout the entire process. If the topic of compensation comes up, you have to be diligent. Because it is such a hairy subject, often people will make off-handed comments, when what they really mean is, "Hey, I think I am underpaid." Most managers would hear that comment but try to ignore it. They think if they don't acknowledge it, it will go away. I believe when it comes to compensation, you need to be highly diligent. If someone makes a comment of that nature, you have to address, it. You need to take the time to decide what avenue you want to pursue.

If that avenue is, "There is no more money in the budget," you owe that person that information right away. If the person is a valuable asset to your company and they feel like they need more money, you need to at least clarify where they can go as an employee. Sometimes it is as simple as saying, "Look, as long as you are in this position, this is the ceiling." If there is a ceiling there, don't kid yourself and don't kid your employee. If you are truly approaching your business from the value of caring about your employees, you want them to be able to make a decision based on real, accurate data.

I encounter this issue often. I have a really high-performing employee who took a pay cut to come work for my company. She had worked here in the past and loved it. She got paid more at her other job, but she was miserable. When a seat opened up within our company, she applied for the position and stepped back in pay. The issue that created, however, is that she is doing a great job, she's very engaged, but she's constantly asking her manager about making more money. I tried to explain to him when he hired her that she needs to understand this is the framework for that job. She needs to understand that as long as she is in this position, this is where the ceiling is in terms of pay. Well, she takes the job, knocks a home run like we knew she would, but six months into the job she is asking if she can get her pay back to what it was at her previous job.

What you see in strong managers is great communication. They are clear up front, and they are clear throughout the process. He should have said to her, "Hey, look, remember our conversation? We are still within that framework. Let's continue to grow this job so we can compensate you percentage-wise equal to what you were making before." Or, "Let's set you up on a path to leadership so you can make a higher salary." He actually said, "I'll check, let me look." You can't say that if you know the answer is going to be no.

My philosophy is this: When the subject of money comes up, regardless of whether it's a general conversation or it's in your daily huddle or weekly meeting, you need to immediately be DEFCON 5 for an answer. You need to immediately find out if increasing that employee's salary is something you can do. Because the wondering is worse than the no. You have to say to that employee, "You are important to me, and you are important to this company, so I have stopped what I am doing to make sure you get an answer." It has to be priority number one. Because in the situation where the subject is breached, it instantly becomes the only thing they are thinking about. We want that to be the last thing they are worried about. The highest priority should be figuring out how to do a great job and make the company better, but that can't be their focus if they are thinking about money. The sooner you get that resolved, whatever the outcome, the better. And if the answer is going to be no, let it be no quick.

If the subject comes up, I am not going to lie or hide from it. I will look them in the eye and face the subject head-on. "Here is what you are doing, here is what you need to do in order to get to the salary you want." I try to get to a place where we agree before they leave that conversation. "Can you see the steps you need to take to reach the salary you want? Because the number you are at now is not going to change as long as you are in this position."

When I bought a new store and promoted one of my employees to general manager, the first thing he thought about was, "I know what the general managers at the store I came from are making, and it is a lot more than what I'm making." I showed him when we started exactly what it was going to take to reach that income level, and he could make the decision to take a more secure compensation with a smaller percentage of the profit, or he could figure out how to get the new store to a point where it was competitive with the other businesses. He was smart and took the higher compensation with the more risk, and now it is paying off dividends.

It is a real conversation. Did I want to have that conversation? No. But at some point, I had to look him in the eye and say, "You have to understand this job pays this much money. If you want it to pay more, you have to make it do more. And if you do that, it will pay more."

I had another employee come into my office the other day. He said, "Hey. I'm looking at these two stores, and their performance is very similar. The expenses are the same, and I can't see where the profit is different. I am wondering why their income level is larger than mine by a substantial amount."

I broke down the financial statement with him because I wanted to get that question off his mind as quickly as possible. I put aside work for a convention that I am the chair of because I knew we needed to go through it immediately. I wanted to eliminate the thought of pay from his mind so he could focus on his job. I showed him in 10 minutes exactly what his opportunity was and how he could get it. He left my office smiling and tickled to death.

My daughter has an employee at her bakery who is superhuman. She does a great job, and she does it because she likes the work, not because she needs the money. But she is a very conservative person and has been around business all her life. It frustrates the heck out of her that my daughter doesn't block employees out of the success of the business; she lets everyone know what the business's revenue is.

My daughter learned this from me. I completely believe that today's businesses need to be transparent, to the point that I like for my managers to compare the financial reports for their section of the business to their counterparts in our other stores. It creates healthy competition. I want them all to be wearing the same brand, I want them all to be united under the Hiester organization, but I also want them to strive to be the very best that they can be. That is part of our core focus.

I am completely transparent when it comes to the profitability of our departments within our business. I want them to understand what makes the business money, so they can contribute to helping it make more. I am clear with them that profit follows performance. If your job generates profit for the company, you are going to be well compensated. But again, money is the factor that takes the employees' minds off the general success of the company, so the faster you can resolve that issue, the more beneficial it will be to them.

The days of hiding your company's success or failure are over. Historically, you weren't supposed to see anything outside of your position, it was thought to be none of your business. Any money the company made or lost was kept secret. I don't believe employees should be siloed in their positions; I want them to be a part of the success or a part of the failure of the company. This is thinking outside the boss. It is accepting new ways of doing things because it is what is in the best interest of your employees, and because of that, your success.

The more real you can be with your employees, the more they will trust you. And most often the error comes from an unrealistic view. Weak managers are afraid if employees see you making a lot of money, they will ask for a raise. And if they see you are doing poorly, they will leave. But these are weak interpretations. You have to trust that what you do and what you say is enough. Your employees knowing the real financial situation of your business is key to your success, not to your detriment.

If you are fair in how you compensate your employees, if you have done your research, know your market, and know what the position should pay, then compensation shouldn't be an issue. I know that 90% of the time it becomes an issue when your employees are frustrated with what they are doing, when they don't see a direction for their career, or they have not bought into the vision. That is when they turn to pay. The truth is, in today's climate, someone will always pay them more. It doesn't matter what they do, someone will pay them more. Right now, there are more jobs than there are people to fill them. This creates a climate where someone will always pay more.

> *You have to trust that what you do and what you say is enough. Your employees knowing the real financial situation of your business is key to your success, not to your detriment.*

I know this: No matter what your business is, once people start focusing on the money, they usually only focus on the money. It doesn't build loyalty or community. None of those things can happen when the focus is on money. I assure every person who comes to work for me that I am going to be fair to them. "If you help the company make money, you will make more money." But it shouldn't be the focus. Some of our employees make more than their counterparts across the industry, and it is because they are not thinking about the money. They are thinking about their quality of work and, as a result, they are rewarded. The money is always a trophy, never the reason they do the job.

IDENTIFY, DISCUSS, SOLVE

In our company, we do something called IDS. We identify, we discuss, and we solve issues.

When the COVID-19 pandemic began, the service manager brought to my attention that the mechanics were concerned about what they should do. They were running out of work halfway through the day, customers weren't leaving their houses, and our service was basically cut in half. We got together in a round table meeting and one of my mechanics said, "Mr. Hiester, what are we going to do when we run out of work halfway through the day? We're paid based on the jobs we accomplish, not on the hours we work. If there are no jobs, our pay is going to be cut in half. Do we go on unemployment? Do we have paid time off? What do we do?" These were really good questions, and I didn't have answers for him.

Management stepped back as a group and said, "What are some things we could do?" We started thinking about how we could keep our employees engaged in working and being paid when they were running out of work halfway through the day.

The idea hit me. What if we bought classic cars, and we paid them to work on those halfway through the day, the same way a customer would pay them to work on their car. That way we would be getting some gain from the appreciation of the value of the vehicles, and we could still pay them the same way they would be paid to work on a customer's vehicle.

Well, the idea morphed. We continued to talk about it, and some of the guys said, "Well, hey, let's make it a contest. Let's have them put two or three mechanics together on a team to work on one project, and the ones that make the biggest difference in the vehicle, we'll auction that vehicle off for charity, and we'll be able to do some good and make it rain in other people's fields." Crazy enough, we bought 19 cars when it was all said and done. We put 14 in the contest, and it became a morale booster.

It was an amazing experience for so many reasons. One was getting to witness the teamwork and camaraderie. There is so much respect that the modern-day mechanic has for the old timer because of his knowledge of the field. It was also beneficial to the goodwill of the company because all of our employees appreciated that when faced with an adverse situation, we didn't run and hide or seek the easiest way out, we found a way to accommodate all parties. Because of it, the reputation of our dealership grew and put us in a position to attract harder-to-find employees like technicians. They saw that we were a company that took care of our people.

It actually got picked up by local television, and they did stories on it. We had mechanics calling us from other dealerships that were laying off their people or just loved the story and felt the passion and the love we had for our employees. They then said, "I want to work for that company." Or, "I want to work for a company that looks at their people in that way, resourcefully trying to find a way to keep them employed, fed, and busy."

One of my vendors and close friends is a manager at Allied Bank. He came to me one day and said, "Hey, we're working on a project at the bank, and I think your story would be a good fit for it. Do you mind if I share it with them? There may be some national opportunity."

I said, "Absolutely."

Sure enough, it got picked up by a national deal with Counting Cars, which is a show that's been on the History Channel for 12 years. We did a miniseries of 22 episodes, and our mechanics got to be in those episodes.

We also allowed the winning team to influence the decision of where we would donate the proceeds from the winning car. We selected five or six North

Carolina organizations that had been impacted by COVID-19, and the winning team got to choose who received the funds. The mechanics that worked on the winning vehicle saw the value in what Military Missions in Action does both in our community and globally and thought it was a great cause. We ended up giving the proceeds to Military Missions in Action. It was especially meaningful because we learned they were short of their budget this year and were deeply concerned. Our donation helped them meet some of their deficiency through the pandemic. It provided a bright light in an otherwise dim year.

Obviously, not all problems we solve through IDS have such exciting solutions, but it illustrates the impact we were able to have through this method.

In my industry, there is a national shortage of skilled employees. Now, this is a non-industry-specific book, so when you think about this, the same can be said for heating and air conditioning, electrical, whatever your business may be. All across the country, there is a shortage of skilled tradesmen. Well, mechanics are the skilled tradesmen of the auto industry. They are aging out, and there is not a large group behind them learning the skills to take up that position, creating a shortage of young, skilled tradesmen.

I serve on the board of the North Carolina Automobile Dealers Association (NCADA), and one of the big topics we hear from every dealer in the country is what are we going to do about this shortage?

Yet we're not experiencing the significant shortage that other dealers are. One of the reasons for this is that when this pandemic hit, and we were running out of work halfway through the day, we didn't take one of our most powerful assets and lay it off. We said, "How are we going to keep them working?"

In the industry, it created a buzz that has put us in a positive position to recruit. We had several mechanics reaching out to us from all over the area wanting to come to work for us because they saw through COVID-19 how we went out of our way to care for our employees.

Is repairing classic cars going to work in every business? Certainly not. But no matter the industry, you can take that practice of IDS to your employees and accomplish greatness through it. When there are issues that arise in your business, you need to step back and identify the issues, discuss them with your team, and come up with a solution that is mutually beneficial for you and your employees.

IDS is one of the most effective ways you can think outside the boss. Firstly, it takes a leader who is willing to think outside the boss to identify the problems that their employees are facing. Too often, management becomes so concerned with their own decisions and responsibilities that the concerns or struggles their employees are facing become invisible to them.

Secondly, it takes someone who is willing to trust a perspective outside of their own to assemble their team and bring that problem to them. Thinking out-side the boss does not mean you are obligated to make every decision on your own.

Lastly, when deciding on a solution, you consider how it will affect your employees and if it will be beneficial to all parties. You are not solely thinking about your own interests, but the interests of your employees. Implementing IDS into your decision-making process allows you to not only make decisions that benefit the company and employees alike, but develops your ability to empathize and understand what your employees' strengths, challenges, and needs are. Once you understand these, you can use that knowledge to inform your recruitment practices.

CHAPTER 9

IT STARTS WITH A VISION FIRST

Upon first glance, it may seem silly to end a book with a chapter relating to the first step of the business journey. But if you have reached this point, I hope you understand that the vision does not end with opening your first store or hiring your first employee. The vision is what keeps you and your employees coming to work every day. It is what keeps them on your team when a competitor offers them more money. It creates the unified work ethic that is guaranteed to make your business a success.

This book has been about me and my business, but it has also been about my employees, my daughters, and my friends. It is their stories as well as mine that have made this book what it is. I wanted something different for this chapter; I wanted this final chapter to provide you with the motivation you need to grow your business.

I wanted to write this book because I felt I had some valuable advice and practices to share in regard to hiring. But my larger goals in life, to inspire, to motivate, to help people become the best version of themselves, have also been present. This chapter is my last chance in this book to do that. And just like in an interview, I am not going to let you leave the room until I have sold you on the vision. Your vision.

THE POWER OF BELIEF

If I were to wake up tomorrow and find myself broke, my business vanished, my wealth depleted, how would I start again? How would I begin hiring? A lot of people find themselves in this situation. You're just starting a business, and you have a great idea, but you need help to accomplish your mission because your company hasn't started to produce anything. What do you do?

To me the answer is obvious. You need to have a vision that is strong enough. You need to have a map of how you are going to achieve that vision. You need to have all the steps clearly laid out, the timelines and success measurables put in place.

Having these systems in place is crucial to any business plan because it creates accountability. This does two things: Firstly, if you go outside of yourself for financial support to help kickstart your business, it allows your investors to have a measurement of accountability towards you. They know that any investment has a risk attached to it, but if you continue to hit your timelines and success measurables, they have peace of mind when it comes to the overall vision.

A lot of people don't do this because the second thing it accomplishes is it holds you accountable to yourself. It is much easier to avoid being held accountable when your goals and plans are vague and unformed. Having no vision—and no measurables—means you are never really failing, but it also means you are never really succeeding. However, defining your goals for your company, where you see it going, and how you plan to get there allows you to regularly reevaluate and reconsider your methods, making sure you continue to hit those measurables and are on the right path. Without these systems put into place, you are just charging up the mountain with little sense of whether you are actually hitting your measurables, if you need to do something different, or if you need to adjust your thinking.

Nobody wants to fail, and so many people consciously or unconsciously will not document their goals in this way out of fear of having tangible proof that they failed. But I believe that the act of writing down these goals and planning for their eventuality in the short term increases the likelihood of success. Your goals and ambitions will make themselves available to you once you identify them.

Ashley's bakery has been such a success that she has run out of space in her current location. It became clear that if the business was to continue to grow at its current pace, they would need more kitchen space. I sat down with her, and we talked through her options: she could either expand the current space by buying from the place next door, she could add another business, or she could move. We spoke with the business next door to ask about buying some of their space, and a few days later one of their people came back to us.

> **Your goals and ambitions will make themselves available to you once you identify them.**

He said, "I was just talking to a customer, and I don't know if you know this, but they are getting ready to put in a whole new shopping center across the street. There are parcels over there for restaurants."

I took a drive over to where the new shopping mall would be and wrote down the number on the sign, gave it a call, and asked them to sit down with Ashley and me. Sure enough, now they're pursuing Ashley to build a brand-new bakery over there.

Choosing to run a business means that you take accountability for the success and well-being of people outside of yourself. Yes, we wanted more space so Ashley's business could run more efficiently, but she also had an obligation to her employees to do what needed to be done to ensure the success of the business. By taking the initiative to find more space, she was holding herself accountable to the responsibility she had for her business and her employees.

The point of this is that this would never have happened if she hadn't taken the time to identify what she wanted and what she needed for her business to succeed. If these things are not clear and documented in such a way that holds you accountable, your vision is not strong enough. It is not enough to simply say where you want to be in five years. You have to also understand where you want to be in six months and how that goal is going to help you get to your five-year mark.

In some cases, if you have a financial goal for six months and end up exceeding it, that investor may even say, "Hey, look, let's make a larger investment because you are surpassing the expectations we put in place." I can tell you from firsthand experience that when you draw a map, when you make a clear plan of what you are trying to do, and you exceed it, it gives the people around you priceless confidence, and it brings the things you desire into your life.

By setting and meeting short-term goals, you identify what your company needs to accomplish at every step in order to meet those long-term goals. This isn't purely monetary, it's developmental as well. You not only believe in your vision, but the people you're considering completely buy in and want to be a part of it too. They have to believe in why you are doing this.

It also builds confidence in the employees you brought on in the beginning. If they see measurables being hit, they can feel secure in knowing they made the right decision by coming to work for you. Even if they aren't making as much money as they could, seeing the expectations you set being met and surpassed gives them credibility in their decision to hitch their horse to your wagon. When they see you holding true to the goals you established in the beginning, it builds trust and confidence that you are doing what you said you would.

This applies to any field. If you're working on developing medication that will change the lives of diabetic patients, that goal needs to be ingrained in everything you do. You need to have a good *why* and a good *how*. If you have a good reason *why* you are doing what you are doing and *how* you mean to accomplish it, you can sell people on *when*. It doesn't matter if you don't have the money to pay an amazing salary now, because you have the evidence to show people *when* it will happen. Yes, money is a factor. People need to be able to pay their bills. But it isn't the end all be all when you have people's hope, faith, and trust. These

> *Money is a factor. People need to be able to pay their bills. But it isn't the end all be all when you have people's hope, faith, and trust.*

are the three words that will guide your business in those early days before you start making money.

How do you build faith? Faith starts with the vision. The vision is what you are going to accomplish and why you are going to accomplish it. The hope comes from what each individual's opportunity is going to be in this business. It is the hope that this risk they are taking will yield opportunities for them. In other words, does what I do matter? Do I have a voice? Am I growing?

The vision should sell your employees on those first three fundamentals. The employees are a part of it; if you're considering hiring them and you don't have any money, all you have is the vision. They have to be completely bought into your vision in order to hope that the opportunities will be there. It comes from their trust in you. If they are going to hook their wagon to you, they need to believe that you believe. They have to believe that you are intuitive enough, hard-working enough, and smart enough to accomplish what you are setting out to do. I don't even think it is that different if you have money. The only difference is it becomes mandatory if you don't have money because you don't have the option to buy people into the vision. A successful businessman still has the hope, faith, and trust of their employees, they just also have the money to back it up.

Again, think back to the first three of the Four Fundamentals. Does what I do matter? Do I have a voice? Am I growing? If you're starting a new venture, growth opportunities are going to be tremendous. Most people on the ground floor of any new venture understand opportunity. Will they lose sight of it? Yes, but only if you don't have clear measurables on what your business is going to be, when you are going to be there, and how to know when you are headed in the right direction.

The first question I would ask myself is: What is my business plan? That business plan must have explicit, tangible goals. It should state what is going to happen 10 years from now, 5 years from now, 3 years from now, or even 1 year from now.

In this exercise, I like to begin with the 10-year goal; this is your big, hairy, audacious goal. It doesn't have to be planned out to the nth degree, but at least having a macro idea of where you want your business to go is critical. From there, I plan out the smaller, more manageable steps to get there. If I am going to reach 10 years, what needs to happen at year five, at year three, at year one? What can I do today to move me towards my big, crazy, 10-year goal? The goal of this exercise is so that when you hit those smaller points, you can identify what you need to do to keep your company on track to reach the 10-year expectation.

For example, let's say we're at a few million in gross revenue today. I know that 10 years from now, my anticipation is to double that in annual revenue. Every business is going to be different, but the goals follow a similar progress. Maybe you're starting a trash company, and you want to have 100 houses that you're picking up trash at in the next two years. How many houses should you be servicing in six months, one year, 18 months? What needs to happen at each of these smaller stages to make that larger goal a reality?

You identify those goals, and then the means through which you can achieve them. In order for our garbage company to reach X more houses, we are going to add Y trash dumpsters. You have to dare to dream big for the far future, while still setting tangible goals for the near future. The first-year goals need to be realistic. Here's what our expectations are, here's what we're trying to get to, here's how we're going to fund this thing when we get there.

Years ago, my company was struggling with capital, and so I went to go find some investors. I went to them and put myself first in the deal. I told them, "We will risk my money before we risk your money." I laid out exactly how we were going to get there, what intervals would be crossed, and the dates by which we would have accomplished our goals. I ended up with a list of people who wanted to invest.

I can assure you this: If you are a trustworthy person and you are passionate about a vision that is thought out with intervals, measurables, and success metrics, there will be people in line to invest in you today. I don't care how old you are, if the cause is good, if your *why* and *how* are good, if your path to get there is clear, people will trust you. And if they trust you, they are going to want to invest in you. This applies to your employees as well. They are making an investment in your vision and future.

In many ways, raising money is the same practice as raising employees. You have to do the same things: sell them on the vision first, get a buy-in from them, and keep them. You get ownership from them for their investment in intellectual property. When I help design a certain piece of your business, whether you pay me or not, I become a part of it. That feeds my desire to grow and be better within your company. This allows your employees to add to your business through their own ideas and experiences.

> *If your path to getting there is clear, people will trust you. And if they trust you, they are going to want to invest in you.*

No matter how talented they are, your employees will never be successful if you don't know what your vision for their success looks like. In that same vein, you can't go out and try and attract quality people for big wages, let alone for free, if you don't have a clear path that you're going to take them on.

This directly relates to the way I understand my position as well. The way I see my role is I am the visionary for the company. I have management and leadership positions at every level of our business.

They are the day-to-day operations managers.

My job is to make sure that everybody's moving towards the core focus and the core vision, which I have established from the beginning. Sometimes that involves staffing levels. Sometimes that involves seeking new opportunities for the people that we have in our organization that have grown to a level where they need other opportunities. Those are really my big jobs.

We establish our core values as a company, and my job is to make sure that every manager in this company lives up to the promise that I make. When the company first started, it was a unit we used to measure who could be here and who fit. But after a while, it became the promise to the people coming here that we're going to surround you with people that embody those characteristics. I need to guard those characteristics.

What do you do when you want your business to win? Well, it starts with you believing. If you don't have a vision that's clear and you don't have a goal that's 10, 5, 3 years down the road, how are you going to convince somebody else that they are making the right decision, that hooking their horse to your wagon is going to make their life better somehow?

Henry Ford once said, "Whether you think you can, or you can't - you're right." It comes down to the power of your belief.

A while back, my golf game was suffering. I called a friend and said, "Hey, I'm struggling. I suck at golf. I need help."

"The first thing you need to do is stop saying you suck, because you don't suck. You probably have some things you need to work on, but start by not telling yourself you suck. We're never going to say that again."

I went out later that week, and I thought about what they said. I started thinking about what I was good at, stopped overanalyzing, and shot one of the better rounds in a long time.

I was so pleased with myself, and I realized that it was all because of my mindset. At the end of the day, it was me versus me. I was competing against myself. I played well because I believed I could. If you believe in yourself and your business, others will too.

BOOK STUDY

As a company, we have our core values, our core focus, and our mission statement. One of the things that is consistent throughout all of them is that we want to ensure the people we come in contact with can be the very best they can possibly be. In a meeting one day, the question came up of what we were doing to invest in the lives of our staff. How are we making them the very best they can be?

Throughout my life, one of the things that helped me more than anything else was reading and listening to leadership books. I grew up on authors like Earl Nightingale, Brian Tracy, and Lou Tice. They helped shape the way I think today. I wanted to motivate my staff to see the value in these books too.

As we talked about it, the idea of a book study came up. But you could sense in the room that not everyone was interested. People didn't know how to do it or were unenthusiastic about doing it. I challenged my team to do one book. Each team member would get five or six people to meet once a week and discuss the book. I would read ahead to create questions, so they didn't even have to be the reader, they just had to facilitate, like in a Bible Study.

I can tell you, every single person in that room was thinking about how difficult it was going to be to get five or six people to participate. To our surprise, the first book had 70 people involved, and by the time we got to the second, we had 90. We had as many people on the sidelines wanting to be involved.

We don't care what position they're in the company. We'll pay for a meal that day, or we'll do whatever we need to do to support the employees. I told them: "It can be in the morning, it could be at lunchtime, it could be in the afternoon, whatever you choose, but I'm challenging you to do this."

Stepping back now, you may be asking how does this connect to how you work on your business? How does this connect to starting with a vision? Well for us, part of the vision for our company was asking, "For our core focus, how can we inspire our people?" And forming a company-wide study group may sound crazy, but it was something we could do together. Let's study these books, and let's get everybody in the room involved. We're not asking anybody to read out loud. We're just asking you to look at the questions that we have and share how they apply. How can you relate this to your current job?

If there are people out there who have big ideas of what they want to do as a business leader but are unsure about getting buy-in from their employees, my insight is that they may surprise you. When it comes to growth opportunities, there are usually far more people willing to get involved than you might think. You would not believe how passionate and excited some of the people get, especially the people you'd think would be less likely to do it. But at the end of the day, if you step back, everything has to do with our core focus and our long-term goals. Perhaps a company-wide study group seems random, but when you understand the larger vision, it makes perfect sense. Part of my vision for my company was to inspire people to be their best selves. The book study was a way we could do that. When we finally stepped up and made it happen, our company benefitted.

If you are like me and are committed to making the people around you the best versions of themselves, you cannot let fear stop you. You never know how many people are looking for opportunities to grow, and whether your ideas might be the perfect tool to help them achieve that growth. Our book study did so much more than help educate our employees; it brought them together and it created unity.

DO IT NOW

My daughter Ashley graduated from North Carolina State with a communications degree. After graduation, she got a job in marketing at a great company. Initially, this seemed like a good fit for her. She had a concentration in marketing, and she took this job straight out of school. She met some great people and learned a lot, but over time, it became clear she was unhappy sitting behind a desk, typing all day. I don't want to imply that there is anything wrong with this kind of work, there certainly isn't. But Ashley has a huge personality, she's a real people person, and it just became clear this wasn't satisfying her in the way she had hoped it would.

Both of my kids are doers. If there is something they want, they will find a way to get it done. When she came to me for advice, I asked her, "Well, if you could do anything you wanted to do, what would you do?"

She said, "Well, you know, at some point in my life, once I've made enough money, I'd love to have a coffee shop and pastry place."

My immediate response was, "Well, why would you wait?"

She was a little hesitant, of course, saying, "I don't know, I just..."

"You know, you're young," I said. "You're not married, you don't have kids. If you're ever going to do it, you don't have a better time than right now."

We started discussing it, and we realized that because of the pandemic, there might actually be places available. Then I realized at that point that I was pushing her a little. I do this in life and business, and I don't want to be pushing her in a direction that she doesn't want to go. I laid back and dropped it for a little bit.

Well, not long after she sent me a picture or two of some coffee art and wall decor. It became clear she was really interested in this. We drafted a letter and sent it to all the coffee shops in the area. It said, "If you have ever thought about selling your business, Ashley has just graduated from State, she's got some culinary experience, and we'd love to talk to you." We sent it to all the coffee shops that she had looked at and was interested in.

Sure enough, two or three of them responded almost immediately. I also saw an online broker had put up a listing for a coffee shop. I reached out to him and told him about her situation.

He called me back and said, "Hey, listen. I don't know where she wants to be, but if she would consider Holly Springs, I've got a fantastic lady who's run into every complication she could starting her business, and once she got it up and going, it was starting to do well and then COVID-19 hit. I don't think she's going to reopen," he said. "It's got fairly new equipment in it, and it's in good shape."

"Well, let me talk to her," I said. I asked Ashley if she wanted to meet me on her lunch break at the bakery.

At the bakery, she looked at me and asked, "How would I do it?"

We talked through the process, and she said, "If you're asking me would I rather be running a coffee shop or doing what I'm doing now, there's no question. I'd rather be running a coffee shop."

I said, "Well, it sounds like you've made your decision." And now she owns that business.

There are things right now that you're putting off doing; everybody has those things. There are goals whether in your personal life or business that you want to achieve but don't know how to begin.

When I talk about your vision, I mean that most people know in their hearts and minds what they'd like to do, but sometimes it seems unrealistic. Sometimes all you need to do is take the time to prepare the details, tangible goals, and how the steps you take every day could make that vision a reality.

Ashley had this dream of owning her own bakery for a long time but didn't feel confident enough to pursue it. Through the process of making that dream a tangible plan, she realized now was the perfect moment for it to happen.

This book study was something I wanted to do for years. These business books had radically changed the way I thought and behaved, and I wanted them to help others too, I just never fully dedicated the time to figure out how to do it. But my team and I were able to make it happen, and it has done such a fantastic job of helping unite our business, that now

I can't believe I had waited so long.

I had wanted to write a book for years; I had wanted to inspire people the way business books had inspired me. I had been working on a book for 10 years.

I challenge my team to create a plan by identifying what would great look like in the department or business they're currently responsible for in 10 years. In order to accomplish that 10-year greatness, what needs to happen in the next three years? In order to accomplish that, what are the most important things to do this year?

We have always done this exercise for our company, but not for individuals and their departmental responsibilities. A lot of people don't see themselves in the same position 10 years from now, so they don't take the time to identify what great looks like that far out. The great thing that came out of this exercise was that even if an individual isn't going to be in that position 10 years from now, a plan is laid out for the next employee who is.

10 years, 3 years, and 1 year. They had to put measurables in place. In order to accomplish that 10-year goal, they had to determine what great looked like for their department. Well, my team consists of general managers, a controller, a parts and service director, an operations manager, and my executive assistant, Brandon. Each one has a unique department, with the exception of Brandon.

Brandon came to me and said, "John, I'm struggling with this exercise. Should I put down my goals for the company? Should I put down financial goals for the company? What should I do?"

I said, "You have to look at the job you're in now. Given what you're doing, what would great look like?"

He said, "Well, I have to make sure the emails are read, I have to schedule appointments." And he continued, "Well, it's about you too. I want you to be a published author. I want you to be an industry expert."

Brandon did the exercise and identified the following goal as encompassing what great looks like 10 years from now; I include this as an example you can use when drafting your own 10-year goals:

"John is recognized by the industry as a world-class thought leader, execution leader, and philanthropic leader."

With this target established, the next question was what needs to happen in the next three years to move us towards that 10-year target. Brandon came up with the following list of items that, if accomplished, could make that goal a reality:

- John is a published author.
- John is the most informed dealer in the country.
- John is called upon to give leadership advice.
- The Executive Assistant position is relied upon as a senior advisor to John Hiester and leadership.
- The Executive Assistant is considered an expert resource on the EOS Model.
- Hiester Automotive Family has created a thriv-

ing foundation centered around kids that is truly making a difference.
- Hiester University breathes spirit into the minds of others.
- A Digital Document Vault is created and maintained with written processes.
- The Hiester Way Dealership Manual is finalized and maintained with written processes.
- The Executive Assistant has a trusted process for daily communications with John Hiester to include emails, voicemails, standard mail, and inter-office communications.
- The Executive Assistant has a trusted process for John Hiester's Business and Personal Calendars with a review process in place.
- The Executive Assistant has a trusted process for John Hiester's Business and Personal Travel Itineraries with a review process in place.
- The Executive Assistant has a trusted process for John Hiester's Business and Personal Files with a review process in place.

We turned to the first item on the list. "What do we need to do this year to make that happen?" I asked.

"I guess we better find a writer," he said.

I can honestly say, if it wasn't for that conversation, I probably would have never become a published author. Brandon had a vision, and he did not wait. He pushed me to do it now. I am proud to say you are now reading my second book because of that.

Whatever it is that you're dreaming to do for yourself or your employees, do it now. Stop thinking about it and do it now because there's no time like the present. If you decide for yourself, as I did, that you want to follow the core focus that you have on the wall and invest in your people, by golly, you need to start doing those things that you intend to do.

> **Whatever it is that you're dreaming to do for yourself or your employees, do it now.**

If I hesitate or procrastinate on what I want for my employees, I am actually doing them a disservice by not living up to the obligation of the Four Fundamentals.

I recently met with a builder and listened to him talk. He said, "Well, as soon as we get this house done, I'm going to go out and use this house as a way to sell more houses."

My point to him was, "Why are you waiting? The proof's already there. You're already building a house, you already have your license; start lining up the second one now. Don't wait."

You're likely reading this book because you're either struggling to hire or you're looking for new ways to do it. Either way, the chances are good you have a need. My hope is that by the time you have finished reading this book, you already have all the tools you need, so stop procrastinating.

Whatever your goals for your business may be, the things you need to accomplish it are already out there. The only thing hindering you from reaching them is your own belief in your success – your ability to sell yourself on the vision. If you have in your mind that you need to do X, Y, and Z, at some point down the road, identify precisely what needs to be done to achieve those goals, break them down into manageable parts, and start now. That conviction, that certainty, is what is going to attract the employees to your business who will be key players in your success.

IT STARTS WITH A VISION FIRST

I'd like to close this book on an exercise, one that I hope will energize and motivate you to accomplish all of your goals for your business. Keeping in mind everything we have covered in this book, I want you to think of three goals you have for your business.

Perhaps you want to hire a larger wait staff for your restaurant. Perhaps you want to begin hiring your first team of people. Maybe you are looking to open a fifth branch of your store. Whatever they may be, select your top three. From those three, pick which one is the most urgent embodiment of your core values. Be honest with yourself, if you are transitioning from a food truck to a brick-and-mortar restaurant, your next goal can't be to open 50 more.

Which of these goals would have the biggest impact on your business right now?

Do you have a goal?

Good.

Now get to work!

ACKNOWLEDGMENTS

Firstly, I want to thank Nesha Ruther for making the process of writing this book not only effortless but fun. She is amazing at what she does, and I am forever grateful.

I'd also like to recognize Brandon Wright for pushing me to publish my books and tirelessly being at every meeting. He put his thoughts and vast knowledge towards making sure the chapters were organized in the best way possible, and all the content was relevant.

I'd like to thank my family. As you can see, they are very important to me. This book would not be possible without the stories and education I've drawn from being a part of their lives.

Thank you to my friends and colleagues who have helped review the book with me.

And thank you to Tim Dagenais for writing the forward.

Finally, thank you to Jeremy Gotwals and his team at Holon Publishing.

ABOUT THE AUTHOR

My name is John Hiester, and I am the founder and CEO of Hiester Automotive. I'm a simple guy. I was born in Ohio. I went to school to be a diesel mechanic but decided to go in a different direction. I got in the car business and worked for Leith in Raleigh, North Carolina, back in the mid-1980s. I worked my way up through the company but got tired of having to move every time they bought a new store. My wife and I were expecting as I moved to work with Darryl Burke Chevrolet in Fuquay. I worked there for nine years before purchasing my first store in Angier, North Carolina, a town of about 2,000 people.

Hiester Automotive now has four stores and over 300 employees in the North Carolina area. I regularly speak around the country at automotive business conferences and am on the board of a number of automotive industry organizations. I published my first book, *Why Jacob Matters: Change Culture and Cultivate Talent by Listening, Leading, and Building Accountability*, in 2019.

Lightning Source UK Ltd.
Milton Keynes UK
UKHW020047221222
414292UK00006B/238